SAFE AT HOME

SAFE AT HOME

Ten Major League Baseball Players
Discuss Their Careers
and Their Christian Commitment

Written by Richard Arndt
Illustrated by Don Kueker

Publishing House
St. Louis

Copyright © 1979 by Concordia Publishing House
3558 South Jefferson Avenue, St. Louis, Missouri 63118

Printed in the United States of America

Library of Congress Cataloging in Publication Data
Main entry under title:

Safe at home.

     1. Religion and sports—Juvenile literature.
2. Baseball players—United States—Biography—Juvenile
literature. I. Arndt, Rick, 1956—
GV706.S22   796.357'092'2 [B]   79-11145
ISBN 0-570-03619-4

To Michael, my youngest
brother

Contents

Acknowledgments

This book was written over the course of the 1977 and 1978 major league baseball seasons with the assistance of many. I wish to express my deep appreciation to my new wife, Cathy, for her support during all stages of the book's development, especially when it was first forming. I also thank our parents and families for their encouragement, especially my mother and father, who took the time to read stories to me when I was young. I thank Thomas S. Tiernan Jr., for accompanying me to Kansas City and helping me there, as well as for his continued support in prayer throughout the past several years. Also deserving of recognition are Danny Wright and Glenn Arnold, who spent long, hot summers with me on dusty neighborhood baseball diamonds when "The 33rd Street League" was in its heyday. Fond memories of my own childhood days on baseball fields served as a source of inspiration for this book. I am very grateful to the King's House and Cathedral prayer communities in Belleville; it has been through the Catholic renewal that Cathy and I have begun to realize the overwhelming love of the Father.

I would like to express my thanks to the St. Louis Cardinal Baseball Club, which is located across the river from our home in Belleville; it was within Busch Memorial Stadium that many of the interviews took place. The American League players were interviewed and photographed in Royals Stadium, courtesy of the Kansas City Royals. I wish to express my thanks to Watson Spoelstra, president and founder of Baseball Chapel, for his valuable suggestions and guidance. I am grateful to Pat McKissack, my editor at Concordia, for her kindness, patience, and encouragement; to each of the players for taking the time to sit before a spinning tape recorder and share his feelings when SAFE AT HOME was only an idea; and to all else who labored with me to produce a book designed to express the profound and wonderful love of God and His work in the hearts of 10 special men.

Finally, with tears stinging in my eyes, I must make an attempt to thank the Father for pouring Himself out upon Cathy and me, freeing us more each day to love Him and His children. We realize it was He, through Jesus and the Spirit, who planted the first seed of inspiration for the book and went on to water it faithfully until it blossomed forth.

Introduction

T he July sun is baking the afternoon earth, and I am walking past a vacant field filled with eagerly chattering youngsters. I pause, unobserved, and drink in the scene before me, hearing the enthusiastic shouts of, "We're the Dodgers," and, "I'm Pete Rose!" seeing the brightly colored, carefully adjusted major league caps, and smelling the faint scent of leather on the clean breeze. The young players are so intensely involved in the game that they fail to notice their lone spectator. After a final glance I reluctantly resume walking, my heart strangely warm. . . .

Each spring and summer day this scene unfolds countless times in towns and cities across the country. Budding baseball hopefuls in the United States closely observe their major league counterparts, soaking in all that they see, absorbing all that they hear. Major league attendance marks have climbed to record levels; in 1978 the Los Angeles Dodgers became the first baseball team in history to draw more than three million spectators in a single season.

Major league baseball players are introduced into the lives of children in many ways; some watch from seats in vast, sparkling stadiums; others sit before the television or page through sports magazines. Major league baseball has blended itself into the flow of American life; today the name of Babe Ruth is undoubtedly as familiar to an American youngster as that of George Washington or Abraham Lincoln. In October the entire nation crackles with the electricity of baseball's fall classic, the World Series.

This book is an open window into the lives of 10 men who play this game. Though all of them have chosen a common profession, each player excels in a particular facet of the game. Some, like Cincinnati's George Foster, have assembled incredible seasons on the diamond, while others, such as Cardinal pitcher Bob Forsch, have had such moments of excellence compressed into a single game. Yet, each of these athletes has something, or rather Someone, in common, Jesus Christ the Son of God.

Each player enjoys a unique friendship with the Lord; some, like Don Kessinger, were brought up in a home permeated with the presence of the Lord; others, such as Bob Watson of Houston, came to know the Father through the example and encouragement of another person, such as a wife or friend. Each, however, has discovered the Good News that Jesus can melt the walls which surround and imprison him, free him of fear and confusion, and fill him with a new abundance of love and peace.

Although, as each player quickly notes, a Christian's life is not completely free of difficulties, a firm friendship with Jesus provides a deep security which enables him to endure the uncertainty of living a life in a world scarred by loneliness and hurt and blindness to the Light of the world.

No athlete in this book pretends to be perfect; each acknowledges in some way or another his own weakness and failings.

The fact that the book contains the stories of only 10 players does not imply that the major leagues hold no more Christians, or that these players are holier or "more Christian" than those not included; these players are simply chosen to represent the many major-leaguers who have found life in Christ.

Richard Arndt
Belleville, Ill.

God is love, and he who abides in love abides in God, and God abides in him.

1 John 4:16 RSV

Doug DeCinces

Third Baseman—Baltimore Orioles

It was Brooks Robinson Day in Baltimore, and every seat in Memorial Stadium held a fan. The Orioles, besides hosting the highly regarded Boston Red Sox, were honoring their legendary third baseman, who was in the twilight of a magnificent career.

For nearly two decades Robinson had dazzled fans everywhere with his amazing play at third base, winning numerous Gold Glove Awards and excelling in other areas of the game. Robinson, however, was preparing to shed his familiar Baltimore uniform, and thus a new player had been groomed to step in at the hot corner—Doug DeCinces.

With his club down 2-0 in the bottom of the first inning, DeCinces stepped in at the plate and looked out at Boston's Mike Paxton. There were two outs, and Orioles were dancing off first and second base. DeCinces steadied himself, then Paxton went to work.

Crack!

His upper body swiveling far to the left, DeCinces watched the ball soar deep into the afternoon haze, grow small, and dissolve into the left field seats. The packed stands of Memorial Stadium erupted into a long and deafening roar, and DeCinces swept around the bases, following his two teammates across the plate. Suddenly the Orioles led 3-2.

"Hitting that home run was probably my biggest thrill," reflected a smiling DeCinces.

The California native, assigned an extremely challenging task when asked to successfully replace Robinson, admitted that the burden had been quite heavy until this September day in Baltimore.

"It was a constant comparison, no matter where I went," related DeCinces. "It was tough. In replacing Brooks, I went through some hair-raising experiences. They didn't want to see me; they wanted to see Brooks. If I made an error or something went wrong, there was always someone yelling, 'You'll never be Brooks Robinson!'"

"They're big shoes to fill," DeCinces continued. "The guy had one of the greatest careers in the game. It took me about a year and a half in the big leagues to realize that Brooks Robinson was Brooks Robinson and I'm Doug DeCinces and I have to go out and play my game and do what I can do and live my style. We're two entirely different people, and I kind of got hung up on that for a while."

When DeCinces' bat drove Mike Paxton's delivery into the seats on that Sunday afternoon, however, he felt as if he had drawn in a deep breath of fresh air.

"Everything was just lifted off me. All of a sudden there was no more weight on me, no weight at all. I had been carrying this thing for too long as it was."

Robinson himself caused no friction throughout this period; his attitude and personality were ingredients which helped to make the transition a maturing process for DeCinces.

"I think Brooks helped me more as a person than as a ballplayer. When he and I were battling, there was never any animosity. I really cared for Brooksie. I felt a tremendous honor taking over for him. But yet, at times I felt I was biting off more than I could chew; the pressure was really tough sometimes. But I lived through it, and I think I'm a better person for it."

Doug DeCinces grew up in Burbank, California, in a climate which permitted him to play sports throughout all 12 months of the year.

"We were constantly playing something out in the street," said DeCinces, who has fond memories of those days. "I can remember Don Drysdale and Willie Mays coming to my Little League on Opening Day. How many kids can have an opportunity to have those two come and speak? I can remember the main thing Don Drysdale said was, 'Baseball is a great game, but yet, you have to go out and play for fun and enjoyment, you have to love to do the things.' And that always stuck with me when I was in Little League coming up; I just loved to play baseball."

Because of his enthusiasm about the sport, DeCinces devoted hour after hour to improving his ability.

"I worked a lot at it, especially when I got to the age where I was 14, 15, and 16 years old. I was playing in three leagues. I can remember a couple of Saturdays when I had a Colt baseball game in the morning, an American Legion game in the afternoon, and a Connie Mack game at night. I just changed uniforms in the car and kept on going; I played a triple-header. My mom loved to watch baseball; that was her greatest pleasure, watching me play."

Even though he played constantly, DeCinces never became bored with baseball.

"I never got sick of it. It was always my dream. It was everything to me to play baseball. I played basketball in high school and had some success at that sport, also, but it just wasn't baseball; baseball was happening. As I was growing up, it didn't make any difference; it was athletics—period. I played football—everything. But there was always that certain special time I devoted to baseball.

17

If it was basketball or football time, I could do other things, but when it was baseball time, it was baseball time. I really devoted my time and efforts as a youth. I look back now and see it definitely paid off for me."

Unlike some of his boyhood companions, DeCinces remained keenly interested in playing baseball as he grew older.

"It's funny, every little kid's dream as a Little Leaguer is to play major league baseball, but it just so happened that I kept the same dream, but my friends slowly but surely kept losing that dream and mine never ceased. I would miss some of the things my friends were doing like going to the beach all the time."

DeCinces' determination bore fruit; in 1970 he was signed by the Baltimore club. When he reached Rochester, an Oriole minor league club, DeCinces played third base for the first time in his professional career.

"That's when I first started being the heir apparent to Brooks Robinson," he said.

During the time he was making the steady climb to the big leagues, DeCinces and his wife Kristi were experiencing a hunger for more direction and meaning in their lives.

"My wife and I came back (to California) after playing a year in Asheville, and we were searching for something; I guess you could say we were really ripe and ready to be plucked. There was another pro ballplayer and his wife; we went to the same high school and were friends. He played for the San Francisco Giants, and he went to this certain church."

DeCinces and his wife accepted an invitation to come to the church, and were later grateful that they did.

"We went to the First Baptist Church in Van Nuys, which is a very big church out there in the San Fernando Valley. It was the first time I had ever been in a church where I heard applause. There was a relaxed, warm fellowship; my wife and I both really remarked about it. We went and saw a group singing, "The Certain Sounds." They put on a tremendous performance, and it was just one of the warmest things. They wrote their lyrics and songs to nowadays music. I never had experienced that before. Then, afterwards, we were sitting around talking, and people knew that we were visitors, and I had never experienced the real Christian warmth like that. My wife and I came home, and we just had a feeling that there was really something brewing, and neither of us had experienced it."

This encounter with a Christian community sent Kristi to the Scriptures, while Doug did some reflecting.

"Immediately my wife started reading the Bible, and she got more into it; but myself, my first reaction was, 'Well, I went to church and through Sunday school and got my Bible as a kid.' She started reading more, and she went to the final Sunday night service."

At one point during the evening, those present were given the opportunity to step forth and receive Jesus Christ.

"My wife got up and went forward," recalled DeCinces. "All of a sudden I was really torn. I didn't know exactly what to do. I had something saying to me, 'You should be going forward, too.' But there was something saying I had already done so as a kid, as a youth. I remembered it, but there still wasn't that certain feeling."

The evening ended with DeCinces still undecided, and throughout the next two weeks he pondered his situation.

"I just kept thinking about it, and really concentrating. I thought of how my wife reacted. I was seeing a great change in her, and I was lacking something; and so, two Sundays after that, I did go forward by myself."

After placing his life into the hands of Jesus Christ, DeCinces, like his wife, began to experience some changes within himself.

"I became more aware of everything. I became more aware of trying to do Christlike things; there was that strong feeling. That was probably my biggest change."

DeCinces emphasized that his inner renewal came gradually; he did not experience a sudden transformation.

"You hear so many people all the time say, 'Wasn't it just like a lightning bolt hit you?' Not every experience is that way, and mine certainly wasn't. I wasn't a rowdy person to begin with, but there

19

was just something else missing. That's the thing I'd like to express; I think far too often people are reading that all these bad people are all of a sudden turning to Christ and getting this fantastic change in their lives and things are just the complete opposite. There's the average person who is leading a good life, but just hasn't asked the Lord to come into his house."

The differences which DeCinces experienced within himself, though not sudden, were deep.

"What I have is His love and knowing that He is with me no matter what I do. Every day that I walk out onto the field, I know He's there with me. There are times when I blow it, I really get upset with myself. I may say things wrong, I may do things wrong, but all of a sudden I catch myself doing them."

DeCinces realizes that the Lord accepts and wants him in spite of his weaknesses and shortcomings.

"I'm not perfect by any means, and I'm not the perfect Christian individual, but yet I have the greatest gift anybody could receive, and that is knowing that Christ died on the cross for my sins."

The Oriole infielder went on to offer an example of how we are cared for and loved by God despite our sinfulness.

"I can remember the teachings I had when I first became a reborn Christian, where Jesus is always up here on the ladder and we're down here, and we keep climbing up the ladder, and then, all of a sudden, we fall a couple of rungs, and then maybe we climb a little bit more, and then fall back a little bit more than we did the first time. Then we climb back up maybe one rung higher on the ladder, but whatever, we're never going to reach the top; there's just nobody on earth who could come close to the Master. I realize that, and I know that even when I have done things wrong and sinned, that I can go and ask for forgiveness, and I have that warm feeling knowing that He's there. It's beautiful, it really is. He understands me; He created me."

DeCinces stressed that becoming a Christian does not mean that a person's faults and difficulties immediately vanish.

"This is probably what non-Christians have a very hard time understanding. They're saying, 'Well, if you're supposed to be a Christian, you've got to walk that white line, and if you fall off, you are a hypocrite.' I've never told anybody I'm perfect. I do things at times which probably make Him very upset with me, but yet, I know He is always going to forgive me. I'm not your model Christian, but what I do know inside of me is the love Jesus Christ has for me."

DeCinces believes that God's love is so tremendous that we, as humans, cannot grasp it totally.

"Oh, it's tremendous!" he exclaimed. "I don't think you can put it into words. It's beyond my scope."

The Baltimore athlete added that in order to experience peace, we must trust in God's love. DeCinces then compared our trust in God with the confidence his own son, Timmy, has in him.

"My son has trust in me when we go swimming; he can jump into the water, swim to me, and know sooner or later I'm going to pick him up. I do give him that delay, because that's how you learn to swim. When he doesn't do it, it bothers me because I feel that he doesn't trust me. It hurts a lot. And so, you can relate that to God— so many children whom He has don't even acknowledge Him; how much that must hurt!

"My feelings of Christianity can be based on family love. I love my wife, I love my son, I love my mom and dad, and there's so much love in there that sometimes you don't express it all. People may think, 'You say God loves me, but He doesn't express things.' But if you really look, He's there."

DeCinces then repeated a story which he heard from a professional football player, something which makes clear how much our Father cares for us.

"I went to a conference, and Norm Evans told me the story. He said, 'I love my son; I love every step that he moves.' He said that one day he stopped by the gate and saw his son throwing the football up in the air. He'd throw it up and it would spin and he would catch it. He decided to throw it really high, and all of a sudden, just as he was about ready to catch it, he tripped. He fell forward, and the spiral came down and hit him right in the forehead. He got up, and Norm said his son didn't know whether to cry or not. Norm stood there, then started to go forward to his son and then he stopped to see what his son was going to do. His son just picked up the football again and threw it back up in the air. Norm said, 'At that moment I was so proud. I don't know how I could love that child any more than I do.' It just hit him; he said—'I don't know if I could do what God did, put my son on the cross for other people's sins.'

"How can we even compare?" continued DeCinces. "How can I even think of His love for us, that He would put His Son through what He did. You don't realize it until you have a son. I don't know if I could do that."

DeCinces pointed out that God has given us each the privilege of saying yes or no to Him; no person can be forced or pressured into surrendering himself to the Lord.

"I'm a chapel leader, and I ask the guys, 'Hey, we're having chapel services. Would you like to come?' Sometimes they say, 'Great, I would like to.' Other times you get that look, like, 'Hey, don't be pushing anything on me.' That alone is probably the worst thing any Christian can do is to push his religion on somebody else. It is your own decision. It was my decision when I was 22 years old, and I got more out of it than having anybody press me into it. I think so many things are being pressured in this world today, that if you're pressured into being a Christian, you may be missing the most important thing."

This doesn't mean, he added, that Christians whom he encountered before his decision did not have a positive influence upon him.

"I look back now and say, 'Well, maybe instead of having driven me away, that more or less primed me.'"

Since the Lord has come into his life, DeCinces finds himself able to relax more easily. This new peace frees him from brooding over disappointments in his life.

'I sometimes enjoy the drive home by myself. It's just that time alone, and then I get home and leave it (the disappointment) at home. When I first started, I used to bring it home, sleep with it, and take it back to the ballpark the next day. It'll drive you nuts! When things are really going bad, it's so easy to slip back into that and say, 'I should have done this, if I had only done this' or, 'I hit that ball so great, but the wind was blowing in.' You don't let it dwell inside of you.

"Some people think what happens out on the field is the end of the world, and there are times when I think it might be. Hey—it's not that important."

Thus, DeCinces spends a great deal of time with his family, and devotes his off-season months to working for his father's construction company in California.

Although professional athletes are often envied, DeCinces realizes from personal experience that those in his profession must live through the same problems and heartbreaks which all people at times endure.

"Ballplayers are human beings, but people sometimes don't think they're human. People think they don't do the same things, that they don't put their socks on the same way, and people worship the things they do. Don Drysdale was my idol; I guess that's part of the game of baseball.

"Can you imagine being down on the playing surface and the place being jam-packed and having everybody cheering for you? I think the youth see that, they relate to that. They say, 'I want to do that, I want to be good enough to do that.'

Although not every youngster has the ability to play a professional sport, each person can receive the most precious gift of all—Jesus Christ Himself.

"I think that the most important thing that I can tell a young individual is to get in touch with himself; don't be one of the gang in doing this. Give God a chance, give Him a chance to at least come into your life. I think you need love in your life, and without God, I don't think you're going to have it, and love is such a beautiful thing, so why not get as much of it as you can?"

23

Bob Forsch

Pitcher—St. Louis Cardinals

It was a cool Tuesday evening in late September of the 1977 baseball season, and St. Louis Cardinal hurler Bob Forsch stood quietly on the pitcher's mound in Busch Memorial Stadium, gazing in at Larry Parrish of the Montreal Expos. The fact that the Redbirds were out of the race for the divisional title, and also the weather, a hint of the coming autumn, may have accounted for the sparse collection of less than 7,000 fans scattered about the park.

Forsch was nursing a 5-0 lead as he went against Parrish with two outs and two strikes, and most fans would have been on their way to the parking lots had it not been that the blonde right-hander was about to become the first Cardinal pitcher in six seasons to win 20 games.

The Cardinal ace looked in past the batter for the signal from catcher Ted Simmons, then went into his windup, and sent the ball humming into the waiting mitt of Simmons.

25

"Stee—rike!" whined the umpire. Forsch, with a look of relief and joy, let himself sink into the crowd of joyful Cardinals which appeared around him as he made his way toward the dugout. The scoreboard became bright with the number 20 flashing and dancing upon it, and the handful of fans roared.

It was a beaming Bob Forsch who stood before his locker in the Cardinal clubhouse as a small circle of reporters engulfed him. He smiled as he answered their questions, which came from all directions. The next day's newspapers and sports shows were splashed with the news of Bob Forsch's 20th victory. It was a bright hour for the Cardinal pitcher.

The next day, during a quiet moment, Forsch sat down and recalled the moment.

"I just felt so good. I knew that I had done it, I knew that I had reached 20 wins. I was just really excited. It's hard to explain. You hear about guys winning 20 games, but you never really think that you've got a shot at it, and then last night I got it."

Only months later, in the early moments of the 1978 campaign, Forsch danced and leaped around the same pitcher's mound after tossing a no-hitter against the powerful Philadelphia Phillies.

It was clear that Bob Forsch was thrilled and proud about his accomplishments. No Cardinal pitcher had won 20 games in a season since Steve Carlton performed the feat in 1971 and Forsch's no-hit jewel was the first thrown by a Redbird hurler at home in 50 years. Forsch was smiling, not only because of these feats on the hill, but because he was sharing his joy with a good friend, Jesus Christ.

This relationship began to blossom during the previous season, when Forsch had a disappointing 8-10 record. The Redbird moundsman feels that the Baseball Chapel services, which he attended with the team every Sunday, had much to do with the deepening of his Christian faith. Baseball Chapel is an organization which helps draw major league baseball players closer to Jesus. Players on each team have a chance to meet with each other every Sunday morning during the season to hear various speakers explain what Jesus has done for them. Forsch explained how these services helped him.

"I didn't have a good season," he admitted, referring to his losing record of 1976, "but I was enjoying the services. I felt that just because I wasn't having a good season, that wasn't the end of the world. Just because you win baseball games doesn't mean you're any better. When you have a bad year, you say 'I'm not as good as I thought.' That's why having a bad season isn't so bad after all. I just can't do it alone. Maybe Jesus was touching me. I had Someone else. I was thanking Him last year for just being there.

"I just felt a strength that was there, and it made me a stronger person. There was just something inside that said, 'You're a better pitcher than that, and if you just stay with it, you'll be all right.'"

Forsch, like anyone, likes to win, but he knows that if he doesn't, he still has a faithful companion in Jesus Christ.

"I guess fulfilling would be one of the best words to use," Forsch said of his relationship with Jesus. "You know you're kind of empty if you don't have Him. Really, there's no void in my life with Him. When things start going bad, I know I've always got Somebody there to talk to, and I know that He's always there. To me, this is the most important thing—that no matter how many things go wrong, regardless of whether it's in a season or in a year or what else, I've got Him and I know that He's watching out over me. I look at Him as being very down to earth. I know the Holy Spirit is always around and I know I can turn to him anytime I want."

Though the Sunday services have contributed greatly to Forsch's relationship with Jesus, it is something which has been with him for as long as he can remember.

"We were brought up in a church-oriented family. We always went to church, even sometimes when we didn't want to, but we had to go. I'm sure it's like that in every family."

The Forsch family lived in Sacramento, California, and attended church at the First Baptist Church in nearby Elk Grove.

"We'd pile in the car on Sunday mornings and go to church

and then go back for the evening service at night. That's just the way it was—that was something that we did every Sunday. You squirm and you talk and laugh with your friends while the service is going on, but really, that's just part of growing up, I think every kid goes through it.

"My mom and dad had the biggest influence on me of anybody. I grew up in a really Christ-oriented home, and I really believe that what you learn early in life carries on later, and eventually you go back to the way you were when you were small. It was just something that was there at home. My dad had his own business, and maybe we didn't get as much as some of the other kids, but we had everything we needed. I just hope that I can bring my family up in the same Christian atmosphere.

"That's just the way we grew up," went on Forsch. "Maybe it took away a little bit from what we wanted to do, but my folks knew it was right to go. My father was a deacon in the church, and we were there every Sunday. We went on vacation occasionally, like any other family, but for the most part we were there every Sunday. Basically, that's how it started, but as far as knowing Him and really realizing that He's there, it really hasn't been until the last couple of years that I've understood and read about Him a little bit more."

The rangy hurler was referring to the time he spends reading the Scriptures.

"Everybody likes John 3:16, and I like that, too. Really, I don't have any favorites. When I feel that there's a need or something like that, I'll just look it up in the reference pages and then read through them. It seems like that works out best. That way I'm finding something new all the time. I read a little bit more of the Scripture."

Forsch also enjoys watching Christian television programs. Both of these, along with the Baseball Chapel services, have drawn him closer to his Friend.

Forsch's partnership with Jesus began when he was a boy, as did his interest in the game of baseball. It was during those years that he played on the church team.

"When I was a little bit older, I started playing Little League in my area. I never really thought of myself as being talented in baseball. I just enjoyed playing it, so I played. My dad was always out playing with us. I just played it because it was fun. I always played shortstop or pitched. The big leagues didn't even enter my mind. I never really had the great aspirations of becoming a major league baseball player until after I signed and got a little taste of it."

Forsch continued to play baseball during his boyhood, and attended Hiram W. Johnson High School in Sacramento, where he began to blossom as an athlete, starring in both basketball and baseball. He was signed by Redbird scout Bill Sayles in 1968 after being drafted in the 38th round of that year's free-agent draft.

"I did pretty good in high school," recalled Forsch. "I had a really good senior year. When I signed originally, the scout who came around said that they thought that they should make a third baseman out of me."

It was at about this time that Bob's older brother, Ken, signed up to play professional baseball—he later went on to pitch for the Houston Astros.

"My folks lost both of us at the same time. We both left home at the same time, and it was hard on them."

For young Forsch, the change in lifestyle took some adjustment.

"I was really homesick," he recalled. "It was the first time I'd ever been away from home, and I had to do everything myself—do my own laundry, do my own cooking."

Forsch went into the minor leagues, still not convinced that he was on his way to the majors.

"I really didn't think I would make it, especially when I was playing third base, because I knew I wasn't hitting high enough. That extra something wasn't there. I was expecting to be released any time. Bob Kennedy, who was the farm director, made the decision to switch me to pitching, so I started working out one spring training in the minor leagues as a pitcher. I went to Cedar Rapids, Iowa, and from there everything started turning out really good. I had been there before. I went back there, I met my wife

Mollie, and I just started enjoying the city and had a great time."

Late in the 1974 campaign the young right-hander was called up from Tulsa, then the Cardinals' highest farm club, to St. Louis.

"I was surprised because there were other pitchers on the team doing a better job. I was throwing the ball pretty good when they needed someone."

Forsch made his major league debut before a sellout crowd in Cincinnati's Riverfront Stadium during the first game of a doubleheader. He allowed only four hits in six and two-thirds innings but dropped a 2-1 heartbreaker. But he was to enjoy brighter days as the season went on, and finished with a 7-4 record and a respectable earned-run average of 2.97. He continued his success by fashioning a 15-10 campaign in 1975, but then fell to 8-10 in 1976, though he did not perform poorly. The Cards managed only a single run in his first three defeats. But although Forsch's record was dismal, he feels that he was being renewed within.

"It just started when I began attending chapel services at the ballpark on Sundays. I just enjoy those chapel services so much, I look forward to Sundays, and so do a lot of guys on our team now. It just gives you a breath of fresh air from everything that's going on in baseball. The faith was always there, but I never really thought about it. Some of the speakers we have are really, really, good, out-standing Christian people, and you can just see the work that's done in somebody else's life and you go—well, they're successful, and yet they've got Jesus working in them."

Forsch knows that his profession as a major leaguer places him squarely in the spotlight.

"Kids really do look up to us. The fans seem to think it's really glamorous. They see it as staying in nice hotels on the road. They see it in one light. I'm sure it's just like any other line of work. Major league baseball is just about how I thought it would be."

Of course, the game of baseball is one in which one day can be a success and the next a failure, and a firm faith in God is needed.

"You know, baseball's funny from a pitching standpoint

because you can go out and maybe be in a really good groove for maybe three or four starts in a row, and then all of a sudden just lose it. The ball feels funny, it doesn't feel like you're stepping in the right direction towards home and all these things. Then maybe you'll throw a couple of games like that and then, all of a sudden, it'll come back and you'll be in a good groove."

Forsch realizes that any athlete must at some time or another face the pain of losing.

"I don't think defeat is any less important whether you're playing amateur baseball or professional baseball. I think when you lose, it hurts. I don't care where you're playing—it hurts to lose and you feel good when you win. It's the same way on this level. The only difference is that you're playing 162 games to get down to the end of the season and maybe winning a championship. There are only a choice few who can say they've been in a World Series or pitched a game in it. To fail along the way is tough, but other people have failed, too.

"Naturally, in 1974, we were right down to the end of the season. I pitched the third-last game of the season and won; Bob Gibson pitched the next night and lost. The next night we were rained out, and our season ended. I was disappointed. I'm not going to say that there weren't any tears in my eyes. But the next season rolled around right after that one, and we started from game one."

The Redbird right-hander not only feels that his faith sustains him, but is not afraid as some players may have been in the past— to express it.

"I think that day is gone," he declared. "Bobby Richardson blazed that trail. I've talked to a few guys on the team. Don Kessinger and I have had some long talks."

Kessinger was a member of the Cardinals during the 1976 season and most of the 1977 campaign. In late August of 1977 he was traded to the White Sox. The veteran second baseman had been the chapel leader for the Cardinals.

"I really, really hated to see Don go," explained Forsch quietly of his Christian friend. "When he left, I had trouble even saying good-bye to him. I got misty-eyed. I just thought so highly of the guy. He was just a gentleman. He was just somebody I could go to and talk with. Maybe we'd sit down in the coffee shop and just talk about religion. I had never been able to sit down and talk to anybody before. He understood the problems that I had, and I understood the problems he had, and it was just good to hash them out and talk about it. It made you feel a lot better."

Forsch appreciates the support of other players, like Kessinger, who share his faith.

"There are other ballplayers interested, and you can sit down and talk with them about Him. He's no mystery man or anything. I think that's what drew me a lot closer to Him—that there are other people around in the same occupation and they're Christian, too. You can be a Christian and still play baseball."

Those are some of the things Forsch tells young people when he speaks to various groups at off-season functions.

"I just tell my experiences—what it's like to play professional baseball, and I just want to get across to them that you can be a Christian and still play sports or be a Christian and do anything. It doesn't matter what your job is. It's just a belief in Jesus Christ, what He does. It's just a fulfilling experience that you have with Him, and basically that's what I tell them.

"I think they enjoy it. I always leave it open for questions at the end. They ask about the guys on the team and things like that—mostly about baseball."

The hurler feels fortunate that he has experienced his share of thrills during his career.

"You read about guys who have attained things like Ty Cobb stealing all those bases, and then watching somebody (Lou Brock) on your own team break a record like that—that's saying something. I can tell my kids about it—that sure, Ty Cobb was good, but we had a guy on our team who was better. Things like that—watching Bob Gibson get his 3,000th strikeout, watching Lou Brock steal 105 bases that year. That's a lifetime experience right there."

Bob Forsch will continue to send baseballs purring past batters, but, more importantly, he will continue to live his life with Jesus Christ.

"He's always been there, and He's Somebody you can depend on."

What then shall we say to this? If God is for us, who is
against us? He who did not spare His own Son but gave Him up
for us all, will He not also give us all things with Him?

Romans 8:31-32 RSV

Jerry Terrell

Utility Player—Kansas City Royals

Before many Kansas City Royals baseball games, as the fans
begin to sift into the team's sparkling stadium, veteran American
leaguer Jerry Terrell spends time around the rails where the fans
gather. Some spectators, crowding around him, hold out
scorecards or baseballs and ask for autographs. Terrell responds
by signing his name, then carefully writes "Romans 10:9" below it.

"I feel if the Lord is giving me an opportunity to write my name
on a piece of paper, the least I can do is to tell the other people
about the message of salvation," explained Terrell. "In a nutshell, I
think Romans 10:9 explains it the best, and so I try to write that
underneath my name on as many things as I can. Even if one
person, through that, receives the Lord as his personal Savior, it's
well worth it."

Minutes after Terrell had finished these words, a small boy,
face alert and eager, called out from behind the rail, "Hey, Jerry, I

looked it up!"

"Good!" answered Terrell, and a glow of pride flooded the youngster's face.

Such responses are heartwarming to Terrell, and he has received an abundant amount of them.

"I've gotten many letters written back to me, and I try to follow them up. They've totally given their lives to Christ, and they want to know where to go from there."

Terrell does this and much more for the Lord, whom he sees as the most important Person in his life.

"The purpose of a Christian's life is to totally give God the glory in everything he does. Kids like to get an athlete's autograph, but rather than give the glory to yourself, give it to the Lord."

Before Terrell's life was transformed several years ago, however, his attitudes were somewhat different. Terrell has spent his major league career as a utility player, an athlete who, rather than start each game, comes in on special occasions to pinch-hit, pinch-run, or to play for defensive purposes. Throughout his career, Terrell has played every position except pitcher and catcher. Yet, before his renewal in Jesus, he felt somewhat impatient performing as a utility man and restlessly awaited an opportunity to display to others his abilities.

"I was hoping that a guy would maybe sprain an ankle or get tired so that I could get out there and play and show them just what I could do. It was always like this, and I wanted to be a starter. I wanted to do good. I wanted all the praise. I was thinking 'baseball for myself, baseball for myself.'"

When Terrell surrendered to God's love, however, this drive for recognition melted away, freeing him to love God and others more deeply.

"It's this 'I' thing, and when you become a Christian, the 'I' thing takes a hike, so to speak."

An example of how the versatile veteran has come to see through new eyes has to do with an early dream of his which, when fulfilled, brought a sudden and clear realization into his life.

36

"The biggest desire I had as a little kid was to have my picture on a baseball bubble-gum card," began Terrell, "and it was really funny, because in 1973 when I finally made the Minnesota Twins, I came in the last day of practice and somebody had put a little piece of cardboard up in my locker and I looked at it closer and it was a picture of me on a baseball bubble-gum card. I thought to myself, 'How shallow are some goals that we set in life.' Here it was, ever since I was a little kid I wanted to have my picture there, and I took it down and I looked at it and I thought, 'Now this is ridiculous; I strove for 20-some years, to get my picture on a little piece of cardboard.' And it really made me realize that there's more to life and that the goals you have in life should be a little deeper than that. I sat there and just kind of looked at it, and I stared at it for a while, and it was really humorous.

"Even though I didn't know it at the time, God was trying to show me that, 'Hey, you've got to have different priorities than that.' The big thing it showed me was the pride factor. I was thinking of everything for myself."

Although this discovery of his own nature disappointed Terrell, it brought forth in his heart a yearning for a deeper fulfillment.

"I was really bugged about it, and it didn't come to a head until one day at our church service."

As Terrell was listening to the pastor, he began to wonder if he had truly given himself to God. If he had not, he wished to make sure that he did; if he had, he did not wish to offend God by doubting it.

"I asked a real good friend of mine who went to church with us about this, and he just said, 'God wants you to know for sure because His love is so total.' Of course, the agape love is what God has for us. He's not going to be worried whether or not you made a decision once before and you were trying to make sure again; He wants you to know without a doubt."

"What God desires," continued Terrell, "is a sincere indication from His child that he is yielding his life to Jesus Christ.

"He wants you to make a heartfelt commitment. He wants you to acknowledge that, 'Hey, I am a sinner; I cannot live a perfect life myself. I cannot handle it myself.' What He wants each individual to do is make that claim: say 'God, You sent Your Son, Christ, down on the cross for me. He rose from the dead, assuring my resurrection.' But I must know Him on a personal level."

Thus Terrell, soon after realizing that God longed to fill his life with a new and complete joy, came before the Lord and totally opened his heart.

"I did that on February 9, 1975," he explained. "I said: 'God, I don't know if I did it at age 12; I may have. Just in case I didn't, Lord, I want to have that right now.' There was no real emotional thundershower, but I had a peace in my heart that I can't even explain."

This new and wonderful security dissolved any apprehension Terrell may have had concerning his death.

"It's a funny thing; I had all the Christian terms, but I still didn't have that assurance; I still didn't know really within my heart, deep down in my heart, that the day I died I was going to be in heaven.

"It changed my complete outlook on physical death, because in a sense, when I made that commitment to Jesus Christ on a personal level, I became spiritually alive. I was spiritually dead before this. You know, they use the phrase 'reborn.' In a sense, this is a good description. Every person on earth is not perfect; he cannot be perfect. But God is holy, perfect, and totally righteous; and He cannot communicate with us completely because we are sinful and God cannot tolerate sin. And so that is why He had to send Jesus Christ as our Savior, to provide a means for us to communicate with Him; a bridging of the gap, so to speak."

Terrell then expressed his gratitude for what Jesus has done for him.

"I really thank Him for it because without Him I'd still be wondering about death. It's so neat when you discuss death and say, 'Well, I'm in the beginning of my eternal life right now; I'm going to live eternally,' and people kind of look at you and say, 'Hey, what are you talking about?' Then I explain to them that I died on the cross when Jesus died. He took my sins with Him at that point, and so actually, my death is done with. I'm finished with death, and the only thing that's going to happen is that my physical body is going to go 'kaput.' When you die, you're gaining, because you're going to be in the presence of the Lord, and the only people who are really going to be sorrowful are the loved ones you leave behind; and that's only temporary, because if they are Christian also, they're going to be with me when their physical death occurs."

Terrell, his wife Kathy, and two sons, Jeffrey and Jimmy lean closely upon their Friend in every area of their lives. As a result of this trust, they have been free to receive the abundance of life which God pours out for them. His presence guides them and provides for them a firm foundation.

One situation through which the Terrells came to rely more deeply upon God arose shortly after Jerry's 1975 commitment.

"It was funny. Two months after becoming a Christian I was sent to the minor leagues. It was really interesting, because I went home and told my wife, and of course we felt bad and we wondered why this had to happen. I'd been studying a book, and it just so happened that I turned to the next chapter and it was 'How to Deal with Athletic Setbacks.' It was just phenomenal, because it was like the Lord was grabbing me by the shirt collar and saying, 'Hey now, quit feeling sorry for yourself; I've got a job for you to do somewhere else.' And as we studied the chapter, we realized that God had a plan for us in the minor leagues; whether I'm even in baseball or not is not important, it's where God wants me."

Terrell and his family thus accepted the adjustment much more willingly, and were pleasantly surprised to find God showering them with gifts through it.

"We went down there and it was amazing, because two other Christians had been sent down, and the foundations for the minor league chapel services started. It was amazing; after the foundation was laid, I was called back up to the major leagues. God allowed me to mature in this little setback. He showed me that I've got to put my trust in Him and not feel sorry for myself. Pride is tough on me."

From this point on, continued Terrell, God steadily worked in his life, helping him rise over a hurdle in 1977, when he was still a Minnesota Twin.

"It looked like I wasn't going to be with Minnesota anymore. We prayed about it, and we said, 'Lord, we realize now that You're in total control. If You don't want us in baseball, that's fine.' At the end of the season we were not with the ball club; we did not know if we were going to be in baseball or if we were going to be pumping gas. We were willing, whatever it was, that God was going to get the glory."

Nine major league teams displayed an interest in Terrell, and when 1978 began, he found himself in the blue of a Kansas City Royals uniform. In time Terrell, his wife Kathy, and their sons, Jeffrey and Jimmy, moved to K.C.

"It's really neat to completely put your life in His control, because when a problem is confronting you, you say, 'Okay, Lord, we want You to take care of this in Your will.' You can put your trust in Him; it's just amazing."

Now that the Minnesota native has come to know what God is really like, this trust flows naturally and easily.

"I would describe Him as the most loving, kind, considerate Individual that you could ever find. God's love for us is so deep that the one thing I would want to convey to kids is how much God loves us."

Though Terrell had always heard of God's overwhelming goodness, he began to genuinely experience it when he himself became a father.

"It really never soaked into me until I had my own boys, and I am going to tell you something: I have never felt a deeper love for any two human beings than for my kids. But the big point is—when I stop and think that God sent His Son to die for me; I could not have sent my sons away to die for somebody; I could not do that. I just feel that I love my kids so much that I couldn't sacrifice them for somebody else. Now, if that is deep love, how much deeper was God's love for us that He did actually send His Son to die for us. It just blows my mind. I can't imagine it.

"You know, it's amazing," went on Terrell. "You hear it over and over, and it really does hit home when it comes to your own family, and I think that's neat. It just shows how much God loves us—totally, unconditionally. I mean, it isn't like if you stumble and falter from the path, He's going to be over you with an iron fist. He's going to pick you up and love you. You find that in all of Scripture. God's love just pours out of the Scriptures. I just enjoy that so much, seeing what kind of unconditional love God has for us."

And, added Terrell, God's brilliant and careful artistry can be seen by a simple glance about.

"Just looking around, you think, God's so smart, just in plain layman's language. To see what He's created—it makes me know all the more that not my will should be done, but His will, because, after all, He's created all these things for beauty and our bodies; He's got to know what's better for us more than we know ourselves. It helps me know I'd better keep my life in tune with God's will; because everything that he has happening to me, whether I think so at the time or not, is good for me. Even little things, even tragedies. You can shuffle away from God or you can plow right through the test and mature in your Christianity. And I think that's what God wants us to do."

Terrell emphasized that while we must cooperate with God by being receptive to Him, we cannot fulfill His call to love on our own.

"Once Christ is in your heart, these good works and moral life will come as a result, because you want to glorify God. You just can't earn your way to heaven. When I am speaking, whether it's kids or adults, I try to make that point clear; it's a free gift from God. Some people have a hard time grasping it, because they've never really been confronted with it. The moral life comes from knowing Christ, and it's too bad it's not known more widely."

Terrell, of course, is eager for all people to experience the freshness and freedom of a life in the Holy Spirit.

"God draws people to Him, and in turn, by drawing them to Him, He will make us available. As long as we stay available for His service, He will draw people to us.

"You know, you get nicknames like 'Reverend' or 'The Straight Arrow,' but giving my life completely to the Lord has really helped. Your teammates notice something different, and they're thinking, 'Hey, maybe I want some of that, too.' They see a consistency, and they watch it. It's really amazing, because once you make a stand for Christ, people really watch you to make sure you're not a hypocrite, and so you've got to give yourself completely to Him and stay walking in the Spirit with Him. You've got to allow Him to stay in control at all times; otherwise you will be inconsistent, and that's the easiest thing to throw a person off."

On top of this, Terrell realizes that some professional athletes may find it difficult to let go and live for God. Yet, these same players, in coming to know Jesus, also come to understand clearly how dull and aimless their lives had been without Him.

"There was an emptiness, there was a shallowness. They could see that they had money and fame; but there was more to it, and it was really eating them up inside. And this was God kind of opening them up to the realization that Christ is the answer, Christ is the Life."

The key to touching others for God, Terrell explained, is to allow the Lord's love to flow freely through our hearts.

"He wants us to always and constantly stay open to be used by Him. We are instruments of God; we're children of God. It's amazing how the Lord will open your eyes, especially when you study the Scriptures and see what God has to say in His Word. It's amazing! It's like unlocking a big door wih His key!

"What an inheritance he's given," exulted Terrell. "It's so unbelievable, it just makes you want to sit up and shout, because you're trying to thank Him for everything He's given you. He's given us so much more than we realize, it's fantastic!"

Thus, said the seasoned athlete, a person who decides to put aside attitudes and tendencies which block the flow of God's life are not really losing anything. Terrell emphasized that when we realize our own emptiness, we can turn to God to be filled.

"You have to be humble," he explained. "When you come to the Lord, you have to really, honestly feel that you can't do it yourself, and it's a humbling experience. It would be simple to just say, 'Well, Lord, take over my life, come into my heart as my Savior,' but you've got to mean it.

"My thrill now is just strictly performing as well as I can for the glory of God, even if it means striking out with the bases loaded. I'm just thrilled to have the opportunity to play baseball for Jesus. In fact, it means more to me now than before, and it meant a lot to me then. But before, I was playing for myself; now I'm devoting and dedicating it to Jesus Christ.

"I think I cheer harder for the guys who are in the position that I would be in on the field when I'm not playing than if I was playing instead of them, because I feel now my job, when I'm not playing, is to keep the other guys up, keep them emotionally high. To be able to play baseball with the talents He's given me is the biggest thrill of my life. He's given me a new attitude."

(Jesus) got up from the supper table and took off His coat. Then He tied a towel around Himself, poured some water into a bowl, and began to wash the disciples' feet. He also dried their feet with the towel He had tied around Himself.

John 13:4-5
The Holy Bible for Children
© CPH 1977

George Foster

Left Fielder—Cincinnati Reds

George Foster, standing in the on-deck circle in Cincinnati's Riverfront Stadium, slowly swung his black bat around his supple frame. His alert eyes studied San Diego Padre pitcher John D'Aquisto.

It was September 28 of the 1977 major league baseball season, and the sturdy outfielder had already collected 51 home runs, chased in 146 runs, and was hitting well above the .300 mark. Despite those accomplishments, the defending World Champion Reds were mired deep in second place, well behind the National League's Western Division leaders, the Los Angeles Dodgers.

Foster strolled to the plate and carefully planted his feet in the batter's box as the San Diego hurler waited. After taking a few sweeps with his bat, he cocked it, raised his eyes, and gazed out at D'Aquisto.

The Padre moundsman worked cautiously to the Cincinnati

slugger, but came in with a pitch that made Foster's eyes light up. He whipped his bat around his chest, sending its barrel driving into the white ball. A piercing crack shot across Riverfront Stadium.

The ball rose far and deep into left field, lingered for a moment, then plunged into the sea of noise beyond the fence. For the 52nd time that season Foster loped around the bases and across the plate into the crowd of red in the Cincinnati dugout.

The only thing that cooled Foster's bat was the ending of the 1977 season, which came a few days later. When the dust had cleared and the ink in the record books had dried, baseball fans everywhere were shaking their heads in astonishment at the season George Foster had put together.

The Cincinnati left fielder had become the fourth National Leaguer in history to belt 50 or more home runs. Except for a pair of 50-plus seasons for the legendary Willie Mays, no National League player had connected for 50 since Pittsburgh's Ralph Kiner hit 51 in 1947. The only other member of this special group is Chicago's Hack Wilson, who drilled a league record 56 and drove in 190 runs in 1930. Other than Wilson, George Foster is the only National-Leaguer since the game's birth to hit over 50 homers and drive in more than 140 runs in a season. During one early-season contest against Atlanta, Foster punished Brave hurlers by corking three round-trippers in a single contest.

Because of this spectacular season, Foster was named the 1977 National League Most Valuable Player. The quiet outfielder had come a long way since his childhood years on the baseball diamonds of southern California.

Born in Tuscaloosa, Alabama, Foster moved with his family to California when he was eight years old.

"I didn't really start playing until we went to California," he recalled. "I didn't play or have the chance to play that much in Alabama."

The hard-hitting Foster went on to explain how he became involved in the game.

"It came about like any other interest in other fields. When you're young, you have dreams to be certain things. You have a dream to do something. You have to keep working at it and believe that it's going to happen."

One reason for Foster's hopeful attitude is that he was brought up in a Christian family.

"That background did help. I was raised in a Baptist church and the teachings from that not only helped then, but they are helping now. It's a part of life. We went to church together. Whatever was dictated in church to do, we did, not only on that particular day, but on every day of the week."

As he grew older, Foster remained firm in his Christian life, and also began to display an impressive amount of talent on the baseball field. After playing Little League baseball for a period of time, he entered high school, and by his sophomore year big-league scouts were beginning to take notice. In 1968, after Foster had completed a year of college, he was signed by the San Francisco Giants of the National League. Curiously enough, Foster was following in the footsteps of his boyhood favorite, Willie Mays, who spent many seasons roaming the Giant outfield and belting home runs.

The talented young Foster spent three seasons in the San Francisco minor league ranks before he was brought up to the majors. It was during this time that Foster began to feel that he could play baseball well enough to stay at that level.

"When I was brought up to the big club, I started realizing that the talents and abilities I did have were enough to qualify me as a major-leaguer. After I had a good year in '69, I wasn't really thinking about being called up, but after I was called up, I really started believing that I could play in the big leagues, and I really played hard and tried to improve in all aspects of the game so I could play in the big leagues."

Yet, after being traded to the Reds and then sent down to their Indianapolis club in 1973, he began to wonder if another opportunity to play in the major leagues would ever come.

"Things started to go the way I didn't want them to go,

because I was sent down. I felt that might be my last chance to play in the big leagues."

Returning to the minors gave Foster time to take a closer look at his life, his goals, and God. Thus, from his disappointment arose a new peace.

"I guess it was a spiritual rebirth," explained the soft-spoken hitter. "My self-awareness was improved, and my outlook on life was improved. So, everything started working out for the best even though I was sent down at the time. It gave me time to think."

This inner renewal happened in 1973, and was the beginning of a fresh attitude for the young player.

"My objective then was to go out there and do the best I could at all times, and no matter how good a game I had that previous game, to try to do better each succeeding game and not compete against anybody but myself."

Foster firmly believes that Christians can use difficulties and obstacles to bring them to a deeper trust in Jesus.

"Things happen to help strengthen your faith. You go through trial and tribulation. That's the reason it's always good to have a good foundation. When things do start going the way you don't want them to, you have something to fall back on."

With a new outlook alive in his life, Foster's career began to flourish. He was brought back up to Cincinnati late in 1973 and remained there into the 1974 season, but saw limited playing time until manager Sparky Anderson made a bold decision. Anderson shifted Pete Rose to third base, making room for his new prospect in left field. The young athlete responded the next season, poking 23 round-trippers and stroking an even .300. He played in the 1975 World Series, in which the Reds edged the Boston Red Sox in seven thrilling games. By 1976 people were beginning to take notice of this quiet young outfielder. Baseball fans voted Foster to a starting position in the outfield of the National League All-Star team. Foster showed his gratitude by hammering a home run, driving in three, and being named the game's Most Valuable Player.

That season the Reds once again cruised to a National League

West title and went on to defeat the Eastern Division champion Philadelphia Phillies in three straight games. In the third contest Foster electrified the crowd by climbing the left-field wall to gather in a long drive by Phillie catcher Bob Boone. That final victory sent the Cincinnati club into another World Series, this time against the American league champion New York Yankees.

Days later the fall classic began, and the Reds continued to play magnificent baseball. Foster hit .429, Johnny Bench .533, and the Cincinnati Reds soared past the New York Yankees in four straight contests. Thus they became only the second National League club since the 1921-22 Giants to win back-to-back world championships.

Foster finished the 1976 campaign with a .306 average, 29 home runs, and 121 RBIs and finished second to teammate Joe Morgan in National League Most Valuable Player balloting that fall. From there Foster roared into his brilliant 1977 season.

Although Foster has experienced many exciting moments on the diamond, the most meaningful of all was simply the opportunity to play in the majors.

"The biggest thrill was getting a chance to play major league ball. I was drafted by only one ball club, and my chances of making it seemed somewhat slim. But the main thing is to get that opportunity."

Thus, since his renewal in 1973, Foster has grown not only in his relationship with God, but as a baseball player.

"The power came with maturity," he explained of his increase in home runs, "but realizing the power along with the quickness came with adjusting. You adjust every day, not only in baseball, but in life itself."

Foster believes that this rapid improvement came because he was willing to develop the natural talents which God gave to him.

"It started as far as birth. He gives you all the opportunities to do what is constructive, so it's up to you to go out there and work toward your development and do the best you can at all times. When you achieve something, try to help somebody else to better his life. Love your neighbor as yourself.

"I condition all the time, all year round," noted Foster. "It's important to try to improve yourself, just stay in shape for whatever particular job or field that you're in. I feel it's an implied obligation to try to stay in the best condition, not only physically, but mentally and spiritually. Not only in baseball, but in life itself I work toward balance. I feel that each person should try to improve himself in all aspects of life."

These are a few of the ideas which Foster shares with people when speaking to various gatherings.

"Being in the spotlight has given me the chance to talk to people, and that's what it's all about, being able to communicate with them," pointed out Foster. "I've had a chance to get through to people of all ages, but mainly the youth, because I am particularly concerned about the youth. They're going to be our future, and they need attention, and they need to be guided in the right direction."

The All-Star outfielder went on to explain that children need to be led down the right paths because the world they live in may confuse them.

"The world is tougher because they're confronted with more problems, more circumstances. It's up to them to make the right choices and to be guided in the right directions. Things are more complex now than before. The main thing is to instill confidence in them, because the world teaches humility. Just let them know about the good and the bad things about life."

Foster also feels that those working with children should realize that each is unique and has been given a free will.

"Each person's tolerance is different from another's, so it's important for the parents or anyone to try to teach or convey to the kids things about life and don't try to keep those things away from them. Just let them know about life so they can select. God gave us a choice to select. It's only right to give your child the same opportunity."

Foster, who also is chapel leader in the Reds' Baseball Chapel services, believes that a Christian stands out because of his life.

"He's different because of the way he knows about life. The non-Christian hasn't been told the things about it."

Yet, he added, more and more people are finding Jesus as a Partner who gives life.

"The trend is leaning toward God. Everybody's been searching and a lot of them are finding. There are still some out there searching who haven't found; but the main thing is they're finding, and it's good to know and good to see."

As much as baseball means to the gifted Foster, he sees his relationship with God as much more important.

"He should be first," he emphasized. "Through Him you're getting whatever you have. You're just doing what you feel you can do. You have joy in doing it, and you have pride in your results. Don't let it become the primary thing in life, because there are other things more important. Give it your all while you're doing it."

Foster also believes that a person who has been blessed with talents should not place himself above others.

"The main thing is to try not to act like you're better than they are. Try to relate to them, not talk down to them; just talk to them like another human being."

Foster, who is careful not to harm his body and makes a habit of giving himself plenty of rest, feels that each person should take care of himself and value the way God created him.

"Just be yourself. That's me. Some might be wild, but I'm just being myself. The main thing is to just be yourself."

When his days as a major-leaguer are over, Foster plans to spend time working with young people, helping them grow in every area.

"I want to go back to school and get my degree in physical education so I can get a coaching or counseling job," he explained. "Maybe not in baseball itself, but maybe in high school, college, or some recreational facility. I feel the things that I've gone through, they're going to go through; and I can lead them along the way, let them know what's going to happen so they know what they're going to be confronted with. I feel that I can communicate with them."

Until then, George Foster will continue to spend time playing in packed stadiums and praying in the quiet of his room. Foster reads a great deal of Scripture, and especially enjoys Psalms 23, 27, 35, 37, and 91 and Romans 12. Because of his firm foundation, he trusts that the Spirit within him is greater than anything he may encounter.

"There are no pressures on me," he declared with confidence. "Whatever situation I'm confronted with I'm able to deal with, because I have God within me. He's within you. He's everywhere."

Thus, because he trusts God, Foster looks with hope at what is yet to come for him.

"You don't know what your future holds for you, but you know who holds the future for you."

When Jesus came to the shore and saw the large crowd, He felt sorry for them because they were like sheep without a shepherd. So He began to teach them many things they needed to know.

Bob Watson

First Baseman—Houston Astros

A stirring wind, cool and fresh from the bay, swept through San Francisco's Candlestick Park. Fans adjusted their windbreakers, and the bright flag in centerfield flapped in all directions. Bob Watson, a member of the visiting Houston Astros, edged gingerly off of the first-base bag, eyes resting on the San Francisco moundsman, John Montefusco. In the batter's box stood Watson's teammate, Jose Cruz. Montefusco, after pausing for a glance at Watson, exploded into motion, sending the ball riding toward home plate, and Watson, legs churning, burst into a sprint for the second-base bag. The throw from the catcher came streaking over the pitcher's mound and into the glove of San Francisco shortstop Chris Speier, who, whirling to apply the tag, was greeted by a sliding Bob Watson. The navy blue arms of the umpire shot out to each side in a "safe" sign.

Watson, banging the dust form his orange and white Houston

uniform, rose again to his feet and crept carefully off of second base. Montefusco returned to the mound, checked on Watson, then poured a pitch in toward Cruz. Moments later Cruz was perched on first base, the result of a walk, and another Houston player, Milt May, stepped in to face Montefusco. The Giant hill ace went into his stretch, briefly watched the Houston baserunners, then sent his first delivery in to May.

May's bat came sweeping around to meet the ball, and before the ringing crack of wood against cowhide had grown faint, the small white sphere had soared far beyond the left-field fence. Bob Watson, his eyes following the ball as it left the park, broke into an easy trot. As he came around the third-base bag, the voices of his teammates called out to him from the bullpen area.

"Step on it, Watson," they cried. "Hurry up and touch the plate!"

Runners who score on home runs are permitted to jog slowly around the bases, and thus the anxious words of Watson's teammates undoubtedly startled him. Though puzzled, he increased his speed, and flashed across homeplate well ahead of Cruz and May. It wasn't until Watson had entered the dugout that everything became clear; when the Houston first baseman's spikes had touched homeplate, his name had become permanently etched into the record books as the player who had scored the one-millionth run in baseball history. Watson had crossed the plate a mere two seconds ahead of Dave Concepcion of the Reds, who was playing in another National League contest on that May afternoon in 1975.

Scoring the one-millionth run in the history of the game is one of the many satisfying moments which Bob Watson has experienced in major league baseball; for more than a decade, the bespectacled All-Star has performed steadily at the plate and in the field. Yet, the Astros have never won a pennant, and therefore have never basked in the nation's sports spotlight. Because of this, many of the accomplishments of Bob Watson have remained in the shadows. Watson, however, has grown accustomed to the fact that many major league fans are unaware of the consistency of his play throughout his career.

"It's been overlooked," agreed the sturdy infielder, "because the Houston ball club has never won a pennant or played in the World Series. Consequently, people don't know what Bob Watson has done throughout the years.

"I guess deep down it bothers me," he continued. "I've done these things and nobody knows about them. But it really doesn't matter; the Houston ball club knows what I am worth to it. The guys on the team know what I mean to the ball club, so that sort of makes up for it. If I didn't know the Lord, I'd probably be very bitter about it."

Any resentment which Watson may have ever harbored because of his obscurity has been washed away by the presence of the Holy Spirit in his heart, following a commitment which he made to Jesus Christ early in his career. Up until this day, Watson's life resembled a tangled wilderness.

Born in Los Angeles, California, Watson spent all of his early life on the outskirts of Watts, a large neighborhood in the L.A. area which was the scene of intense riots throughout the 1960's. From his childhood years on, Watson was exposed to the restlessness and frustration typical of life in the ghetto. Often this tension and bitterness hardened into hatred, and gang wars, looting, and all types of violence broke out. Because of the intolerable living conditions, jammed neighborhoods, and bleak outlook for the future, many youth became indifferent to any moral restraints, choosing to prowl angrily through a jungle of asphalt and chain-link fences.

"I know a number of guys personally who were seriously wounded or killed in skirmishes between the gangs, along with a lot of innocent bystanders," reflected the talented first baseman. "A lot of the guys who I played with are either drug addicts, or have robbed banks or filling stations, and the law has caught up with them. I could have very easily been caught up in that. It would have been very easy for me to be just like the other guys in our neighborhood—be involved in the gang warfare, stealing, or whatever."

Although he refused to become involved in the storm of violence raging around him, Watson was not entirely free of physical danger; he had to maintain peaceful relations with members of every group in order to avoid developing enemies.

"I was in a tough situation," he recalled. "I went to a high school which was in one gang's territory, and I lived in another gang's territory, so I had to play both sides. On the way to school, I was friends with some guys, and then when I got to school I was friends with the other guys."

The pressure on Watson to join a youth gang was intense; but Watson, through his dedication to athletics, managed to remain free of that way of life.

"Sports was one of the things that kept me off the street," he explained. "Baseball was always big in my life."

The sport meant so much to the young Californian that he was willing to squirm through what he felt was a dull Sunday morning church service in order to receive permission to spend the remainder of the day on a baseball diamond.

"My grandparents raised me, and that was one of their rules, that I had to go to church on Sunday if I wanted to play ball that Sunday afternoon. So you know I was there; I wanted to play ball. I went because I wanted to play ball; I really didn't get a whole lot out of it."

Yet Watson, already developing into a solid athlete, came into contact with a man who displayed genuine concern, not only for his physical potential, but also for his spiritual life.

"I had a coach who was a member of the Fellowship of Christian Athletes, and he took me under his wing, along with a number of other guys who played major league baseball—Bobby Tolan and Willie Crawford," recounted Watson. "This fellow, Phil Pote, introduced us to Christian athletics. He gave each of us a Bible, and would constantly use phrases from the Bible. I think he was the first Christian we encountered."

Although Pote had opened a door and brought light into Watson's life, the young athlete had not yet arrived at the point where he was willing to yield his entire life to God. The events in his life, it appeared, were progressing quite smoothly. He was signed in 1965 by the Houston Astros, one of the expansion clubs which came into the National League during that decade, and in 1966 made his first appearance in a big league uniform. By 1970 the young man, who had been nicknamed "The Bull" by friends, had become the Astros' regular first baseman. Bob Watson, a young man from a Los Angeles ghetto, had become a starting player in the major leagues, one of only a handful to maintain a career average of nearly .300.

All appeared to be well in the life of the National League newcomer; he had met and married his present wife, Carol, and at the same time was beginning to earn a reputation as a promising young star. Yet Watson found himself thirsting for something more than what major league baseball could offer him, and was uncertain as to why he felt such a deep hunger. It was during this time that the words of Phil Pote echoed through his mind, and the powerful first baseman began to weigh within himself the cost of abandoning control of his life and allowing Jesus Christ to direct it.

"It was basically because of my wife," explained Watson of his receptive attitude toward Christianity. "She had made a commitment to Jesus Christ a year before. It's tough living in a home where you have one person who is Christian and one who is not. I had not made a serious commitment, and we got down to a situation where I either had to take a serious look at Christianity or I was going to lose my family. I had totally different views than she had. We would argue frequently; she wanted to go to a Bible Study, and I wanted to go somewhere else. She wanted to go over to another Christian's home and fellowship, and I wanted to go fishing. It just wasn't working."

Watson, realizing that he was unable to bring his wavering life into balance, came to the Lord, broken and repentant.

"I had to make a decision as to whether I wanted my family and Christianity, or I wanted to do what Bob Watson wanted to do. I guess I had been avoiding it and also I was in the dark in certain areas."

The Houston first-sacker felt hesitant about entering into this new friendship with a Person with whom he was not familiar; taking such a plunge required both courage and trust.

"I knew I would have to make some tremendous sacrifices that I guess I really wasn't ready to make. I knew I would have to give up a lot of things that I felt I wasn't ready to give up, things that everybody strives for. People were telling me that, 'Hey, if you become a Christian, you have to let God run your life.' You have to make a commitment, not just to God Himself, but to yourself, to your wife, to people, and to your job. I had been used to just going around doing what I wanted to. Hey, I was in the big leagues! I was in cities I'd never been in before, and I made more money than ever before. But there was something missing, especially in my family life and spiritual life."

These thoughts tossed and whirled through Watson's mind for several weeks, and on an evening late in 1972 he took the first step toward a new and abundant life.

"I had come home from the ball park, and my wife and I were talking. I said, 'I'm going to give Christ a go.' I said, 'I don't have anything to lose but everything to gain. What I really would be losing would be you and my kids; what I have to gain is eternal life.' And so I said, 'I have to go along with you.' And we knelt down and prayed, and right then and there I gave my life to Christ."

Immediately following that evening, Watson experienced an extreme inward excitement and warmth, and although this initial feeling gradually faded and difficulties resurfaced, he knew that his life had indeed been touched.

"I felt a spiritual 'high' for two or three weeks," remembered Watson. "but I want to say this, everything from that day has not been all peaches and cream. Since I've made that commitment, I think there have been more trials to test my faith in the Lord than I can describe here. I probably haven't handled them all the way the Lord would want me to handle them either. There have been a number of things that have happened to Bob Watson that have made me grow. A tragic thing happened to a friend of mine, Andy Thornton. He lost his wife and daughter, and I called him to comfort him and he told me, 'Bobby, I am not bitter. The Lord took my wife and daughter away to be with Him, and I know it's for the good.' And that really blew my mind. Here's a man who had just lost his family, and he felt that way. Things like that have really, really made me grow."

Watson believes that although a Christian cannot help but be exposed to some kind of suffering while living in the world, he can blossom rather than wither because of hardship if he draws his nourishment from the Holy Spirit.

"Adversity is the easiest way to find out what you're made of, and when things are going bad it's easy to give in. If a guy at the time when things are going bad can really call on the Lord and pray constantly, he can see his way through without going off the deep end. A lot of guys when they're in the middle of adversity drink a whole lot or take some other drugs or call on something else besides the Lord to see them through their adversities."

It is a wonderful privilege to be able to rejoice for all which is flowing smoothly in our lives, pointed out Watson, but Christians can even be thankful when wading through seas of troubles, for these moments can produce new fruit.

"I've read in the Scripture that the Lord tests you just like they test the purity of gold. They send it through the furnace, and what comes out is nothing but pure gold."

A Christian living in a world darkened by separation from God cannot help but encounter some harshness within it, yet the Father yearns to free His children from inner suffering caused by their lack of self-acceptance and ability to forgive and like themselves. Such obstacles, noted Watson, make it difficult to genuinely feel in our hearts that God cares for us.

"How can somebody love somebody else if he doesn't love himself?" asked Watson. "I try; I'm beginning to love myself, and if I can love myself, I can love everybody. Love is a feeling of compassion for fellowman, trusting somebody the way you want to be trusted. That's one of the things my grandmother and grandfather always told me, 'Whatever you do, trust people the way you want to be trusted.' And I have to say this—I've been burned with that quite a few times, where I've felt I've been trusting somebody else, and I got dumped on and stabbed in the back. But as long as I feel that I'm treating somebody else right, I guess that's what the Lord wants me to do."

As a major league baseball player, Watson comes across many opportunities to forigve another rather than seek revenge.

"The New Covenant says, 'Hey, turn the other cheek,'" said the National League slugger. "Just for instance, say we're playing a game and the pitcher throws one high and inside or behind me. All right, my natural instinct is, 'I'm a man, and I want to go out there and pound on the guy's head.' But in a moment it will all come back, 'Hey, you, get in, go and try to hit the ball and beat him that way instead of physically. Beat him at his own game.' Being a hitter, I don't like anybody throwing at me, and that's something the Lord's really dealing about with me."

As a person draws nearer to Jesus, Watson observed, he feels less of a need to prove and establish himself; he feels secure simply because he realizes that he is a child of the Father.

"It is very easy to have ego running the show, and I am one of those guys who has a powerful ego. I always wanted to do this, I always wanted to do that. Maybe I didn't come out verbally and say so, but deep down in, I was always striving to be the best because I thought, 'Hey, it'll make Bob Watson look good.' Now I'm having a battle; I made a new commitment that I would have Jesus rather than my ego on the throne of my life, and that's the way it's supposed to be. Ego is good if you have it on the outside and have Jesus on the throne."

New life has poured into all areas of Watson's life, gently washing away old and hidden fears and filling in the empty places with peace and love. One area into which Jesus has entered is Watson's attitude towards death; once uneasy about dying, he is now coming to see it in a new and refreshing way.

"In the past I was like everybody else—I didn't want to die because of the uncertainty of what is going to happen. This is something that a lot of people don't like to think about, but it's inevitable. The Lord said, 'Hey, if you believe in Me, you'll have eternal life.' Everything goes through a death cycle. A farmer will plant a seed, and it will 'die' and grow into something new."

Watson, when speaking of abundant life springing forth from the 'death' of a seed, was echoing the words of Jesus Himself in the Gospel of John. The Lord, referring to His own approaching death, used these words, "Now the hour has come for the Son of Man to be glorified. I tell you most solemnly, unless a wheat grain falls on the ground and dies, it remains only a single grain, but if it dies, it yields a rich harvest" (John 12:23-24 JB). Jesus' words refer to more than death of our bodies; for a Christian, through work for the Holy Spirit, dies each day to his old nature, gradually becoming more like Jesus. Watson, realizing that Christianity is a journey, looks eagerly ahead to all which he and his Friend will enjoy together along the way.

"I'm constantly searching to know God better, know Him more," explained the veteran National Leaguer. "The guy who is a Christian always has something there to guide him, if he will let it guide him. I am learning more and more that, rather than falling back on Christianity, I should let it lead me. That's something which the Lord wants you to do anyway; He says, 'Let Me have control of your life,'" Because Watson has placed himself into the care of God, he listens carefully to what the Spirit says each day, and thus is making no rigid arrangements for the time when he puts aside his bat and glove.

"I don't really have a set plan right now," he admitted. "I'm going to live it one day at a time and let the Lord take care of that one day.

"Baseball has given me a whole lot," he continued. "It's actually everything I have. I might work in a program where I can help youngsters know the game of baseball a little bit better and just help them in certain areas, but I think basically that I would like to do after I finish playing ball is continue to grow spiritually. Normally, the transition from ballplayer to everyday Joe Blow has been kind of hard for ballplayers. You're not in the spotlight; you're not making the big money; you don't travel anymore. It's something that's tough to cope with, but I think with the Lord as Captain of the ship, I should have somewhat smoother sailing than most people."

Yet Watson is not the only major-leaguer who has come to know Jesus as a Friend; increasing numbers of professional athletes are opening their doors to the Lord and His love.

"All over major league baseball, more players are standing up for Christ. Watson Spoelstra (the man who organized Baseball Chapel) has done a fantastic job with the chapel program. We went from three clubs to 26, and attendance is overwhelming. The Lord is working in major league baseball and professional sports."

Thus, many athletes, like Watson, have found that even the glamour and fame enjoyed by a professional athlete does not measure up to the comfort of knowing Jesus Christ through His Holy Spirit.

"Money and recognition are things that go hand in hand with baseball," explained Watson, "but I know the Lord, and all of this becomes secondary."

Realizing in a new way his own weakness, Watson, rather than mourning, turns in trust to His Father, whose love, steadfast and firm, steadies him. Because of this, Bob Watson, once bewildered and frightened by life, knows he has been given a home, and is only now beginning to explore its beauty.

"I'm not going to say that I've got it all down pat," he cautioned, "because I don't. But my prayer every day is to help me through the day, to help me love people the way that Christ loves people. And that's all I can do; I let Him take it from there."

Don Sutton

Pitcher—Los Angeles Dodgers

On Friday, July 15, 1977, Los Angeles Dodger pitcher Don Sutton received a phone call. From the other end of the line crackled the voice of Sparky Anderson, manager of the world Champion Cincinnati Reds and also of the 1977 National League All-Star team, which was scheduled to meet the American League All-Star club the following Tuesday evening in Yankee Stadium. Anderson's message was simple and clear, but it was about to send Donald Howard Sutton whirling through the most thrilling days of his career; the talented right-hander was being asked to be the starting pitcher in the 1977 All-Star game.

Tuesday evening arrived, and New York's Yankee Stadium, the most famous park in baseball history, was packed to the rafters. The murmurs and whispers of the fans swept through the stands, for within minutes the annual midsummer classic was slated to begin. Not only were thousands watching from the stands, millions of fans were settling down before their home telelvision sets, hearts pounding with anticipation. Television crews trained cameras upon the field from every imaginable angle.

In the National League bullpen, Don Sutton sent his final warmup tosses over the plate, then returned to the dugout, sat down, and waited.

The classic contest began; and Sutton watched his team-mates, sparked by a Joe Morgan homer, promptly bang in four runs. After the final out the Los Angeles hurler made the slow journey to the pitcher's mound. He kicked at the dirt momentarily, then began to send warmup pitches into the mitt of Cincinnati Reds catcher Johnny Bench, as the American League's talented leadoff hitter, Minnesota's Rod Carew, watched from the on-deck circle.

It was the first time in Sutton's life that he had ever stood on the mound in Yankee Stadium; and yet, as a child, he had dreamed of being there, but in Yankee pinstripes, not Dodger blue.

"My whole life I wanted to play for the Yankees," he recalled. "I couldn't envision myself playing anywhere else. As a kid I would pitch mental shutouts in Yankee Stadium. I must have pitched four or five hundred World Series games against the Dodgers in which I would be the winning pitcher and Mickey Mantle would catch the last fly ball. So when I went to Yankee Stadium to play in the All-Star game, it was a funny feeling—it was like I was totally awed at being there, but it was almost as though I should have been there because I had been there before. Even though Yankee Stadium was changed, I could kind of picture where everything was, and I almost knew how the mound was going to feel. And so to walk out there wasn't as though it was a strange, new place; it was just an awesome place to be in. It wasn't as though it was new, it was just the feeling of finally being back there again."

Those thoughts were undoubtedly flooding Sutton's mind as he watched Rod Carew dig in between the fresh chalk lines of the batter's box. The Los Angeles veteran then went into his windup and sent the ball blazing in. Carew whipped his bat around and slapped a sharp ground ball back at Sutton, who fielded it,whirled, and drilled it into the glove of first baseman Steve Garvey.

Sutton whiffed New York's Willie Randolph, but then walked the Royals' George Brett. Unruffled, the lean right-hander coaxed an infield pop-up from the bat of veteran Boston star Carl Yastrzemski. Sutton returned to the National League dugout, but emerged a half inning later and went on to fashion two more magnificent innings against the American League's finest players.

Sutton threw nearly perfect baseball, although Carew slapped a hit in the third inning, the only safety the L.A. pitcher was to allow during his three-inning appearance. On top of his one-hit performance, the Dodger moundsman fanned four while walking only one. For this effort Don Sutton was credited with the victory, as the National League cruised to a 7-5 victory. Moments later, amidst the postgame words of congratulation, Sutton was informed that he had been voted the All-Star Game's Most Valuable Player.

"It was just unbelievable," marvelled Sutton later. "To start the All-Star game was something I didn't expect. That in itself was enough, but to win it, and then to have somebody come in and hand me the Most Valuable Player trophy—it was just a little more than I could comprehend. It was most of my childhood dreams rolled up into one right there."

These early hopes were part of Sutton's boyhood days in Clio, Alabama, and later in Florida. It was during this time that the L.A. pitcher became firmly anchored in his relationship with his important Partner—Jesus Christ.

"I grew up in a Christian family, which I think was a real advantage for me," noted Sutton. "A lot of kids don't really get exposed to Sunday school and the Bible and Christianity and the plan of salvation. I can't remember when my parents didn't go to church and take us. Everyone in our family was a Christian before I left home. It was a total Christian family, so in that light, it was a very happy family."

It was during his young life that Sutton made a very important decision.

"I knew when I was eight that I was going to play in the big leagues," recalled Sutton of his early confidence. "I didn't know exactly where. I thought I'd be with the Yankees, because I was a Yankee fan."

Because of this sureness, the young athlete was met with a great deal of skepticism on the part of those around him.

"I didn't say that I wanted to play in the big leagues, I said 'I'm going to,' and they kept saying, 'Isn't that cute? He wants to be a big-league ballplayer. That's neat.' But my parents encouraged me, and some other people."

Yet, continued Sutton, the feelings of others did not discourage him; he turned them into stepping stones.

"I have the type personality that all of the negative reactions made me that more sure that that was what I wanted to do and was going to do. It seemed like every time somebody said, 'Hey, why don't you forget it and do something worthwhile?' that just made me all the more determined to be here. Instead of being a stumbling block, it became something I could step up on and overcome."

Thus Sutton spent many hours playing baseball in the warmth of the South.

"Long as I can remember, I have had a baseball or a softball in my hand. I was one of those guys who played baseball probably 360 days out of the year, maybe missing Christmas, Easter, New Year's, the Fourth of July, and Thanksgiving. Other than that I played ball every day."

Sutton began by playing shortstop as well as pitching but devoted himself to mound duties after coming to a realization concerning his abilities.

"I realized there wasn't going to be too much of a demand for a no-hit, no-field shortstop, so I started pitching. My sixth-grade teacher, Henry Roper, was a former pitcher in the Giants' organization, and he taught me all the fundamentals that I still use today. So there's another continuation of a very fortunate childhood; there was a right man in the right place, who not only taught me to throw a ball, but the proper way to do it, and a way that I still use right now."

Sutton continued to dedicate himself to baseball throughout high school and junior college. During those years he endured some inner struggles, yet through these experiences grew to realize his dependence upon God.

"I didn't get knocked off a donkey by a shining light or anything," he began, referring to the conversion of St. Paul. "I think it was a growing process for me, and in the growing process, I did some things that I'm not really proud of."

The Los Angeles hurler went on to explain those events which drew him nearer to Jesus Christ.

"I was dating a girl in high school and her parents told me that they didn't think I had high enough ideals and worthwhile enough ambitions to be a proper person to continue to see their daughter, so would I please not come to their house anymore. That struck me kind of hard, because she was a special person in my life. I was going away to live at a junior college in Florida with some people I didn't know, in a situation in which I wasn't really sure of myself, so I started working to be one of the boys."

Thus Sutton spent many late hours outside of the dormitory, running around with friends until he was exhausted and confused.

"I woke up one morning after a miserable night, very sick, and came face-to-face with myself in the mirror. It was like I was looking at somebody who wasn't me. If I had any large recommitment experience, if I had to say anything helped me turn my life around or gave me a greater appreciation for the power of God, that was that. I said 'Lord, I fouled up a segment of my life and things aren't going well. If You are the God that You say You are and can handle the reconstruction projects You say You can, then I commit my life to You—totally. Whatever happens from now on, it's for Your will and Your glory.'"

From that moment on, Sutton's life began to flourish steadily.

"To oversimplify, it was like a puzzle went up in the air and pieces started falling into place one at a time, from the year at junior college, to getting an invitation to play in a college tournament, to the National Baseball Congress Tournament in Wichita, to signing with the Dodgers, a club I had put 20th on my list."

Sutton went on to list the reasons why he did not wish to play for the Los Angeles club.

"I did not like them. I was totally committed to not playing with them" he declared. "They were rivals of the Yankees, and I didn't see myself pitching with them because most of their pitchers had track records of being six-foot-five and throwing it through brick walls, and that wasn't me.

"But," continued a reflective Sutton, "there was a master plan, and I think because it was out of my hands and into His, that master plan took place. Had I not gone to L.A. to play, I would not have met the girl I married and have the life and the environment and the roots that I have out there. So had it been left up to me to make the decisions, I would probably be struggling on an expansion club somewhere, if I were still playing; or I might be chasing cows in South Alabama, who knows? But because it was out of my hands, good things happened; and I firmly believe it was because God willed it so."

Of course, rededicating himself was only a beginning, and Sutton's Christian life has continued to bear fruit throughout the years. A relationship with God has been the source of many blessings for Sutton, his wife, Patti, and their children, Daron and Staci. Remaining close to Jesus has also steadied his career, but there are deeper benefits which he enjoys.

"One is eternal salvation, knowledge of the fact that you're born again, that you can have a home in heaven and that death isn't the end of everything. We're all human enough that we can't say, 'Hey, I'd like to die tomorrow,' but the knowledge that when I die I'm not going to be just left in a hole in the ground—that's a good feeling."

Because he is a Christian, Sutton knows that he never will be alone.

"Being a Christian assures me that I have Christ as my Partner in whatever I do in daily life. He's a lifetime, genuine, true Friend, who understands and is always there to help. I think too often we don't talk about that; we talk about being a Christian so you can go to heaven, and that's neat. But in the meantime you've got to do something until you die and go to heaven."

As he awaits this glorious day, Sutton continues to serve God through his athletic ability. Though playing major league baseball can be very demanding and exhausting, he looks upon it as an enjoyable experience.

"I've always approached it as if it was fun. I've always played it because it was fun. Even though I do it for a livelihood, I enjoy coming to the ballpark. I enjoy the things you have to do to be a baseball player, such as the conditioning.

"I run cross-country, which is related to baseball in that you have to condition to play, but it's totally unrelated as far as the structure of the game is concerned. I enjoy getting out and running. I run 6, 8, sometimes 10 miles a day. I enjoy that. It's gotten to be a habit. It's really good for me emotionally because I get out, away from the ball park, away from the cities, away from everything and just run by myself. It obviously helps me to condition, but it also helps me mentally. After a while, it's just like flying, like I imagine soaring would be."

All of these pleasant moments were climaxed by Sutton's brilliant performance in the 1977 All-Star game. Yet, more excitement was ahead, for three months later the Dodgers met the New York Yankees in the World Series.

The World Series of 1977 was special for many reasons. For one, the Dodgers and Yankees have been involved in many classic series encounters, some during the days when the Dodgers were still playing in Brooklyn, only a subway ride away from Yankee Stadium. A "subway series" had special meaning to baseball fans, especially those in New York. Thus, even today a World Series featuring these two clubs is a classic.

It was meaningful in a deeper way for Don Sutton, considering that three months earlier he had experienced the most thrilling moment of his baseball career on the Yankee mound and that his lifelong dream had been to play on a world champion club.

The West Division champion Dodgers had fought from behind to shock the East Division champ Philadelphia Phillies only days before in the best-of-five series for the National League pennant. Don Sutton's contribution had been a complete-game triumph in Game Two. The Los Angeles club now found itself facing the powerful Yankees. Dodger manager Tommy Lasorda gave Sutton the starting nod in the opening game, and for the second time in his career the L.A. right-hander climbed the mound in Yankee Stadium.

Sutton's teammates had sent a pair of runs over in the top half of the first inning, and the Dodger ace permitted a single New York run when the Yanks came to bat. From then on, Sutton and Yankee hurler Don Gullett exchanged a string of scoreless innings until Lasorda removed his starter in the eighth. As Sutton watched from the dugout, New York scored a run in the 12th to take the contest 4-3.

The Dodgers surged back to win Game Two 6-1, but dropped the next two clashes, played in Dodger Stadium, by scores of 5-3 and 4-2. In the fifth encounter Sutton took the hill before a home crowd of nearly 56,000 and emerged a 10-4 victor. Yet, the next game saw the New York Yankees, led by Reggie Jackson's three home runs, win 8-4 and become world champions.

All in all, the campaign had been a brilliant one for Don Sutton. During the following season the Los Angeles club once again captured the West Division flag, triumphed over the Philadelphia Phillies in the National League playoffs, and encountered the Yankees in the World Series, and Sutton once again found himself on the mound during October's classic contest. Although the Dodgers fell to the Yankees, Don Sutton had once again experienced what many players could only dream about. Yet, despite all of the memorable moments, the Dodger mound artist expressed other hopes for his career.

"I feel I've accomplished every goal I've ever set for myself except one—to be on a World Series winner. I've played in four World Series, I've pitched in three World Series and I've won two World Series games, so those things are in the past. I said a long time ago that I wanted to play on a world's champion, and if I could do that, it would fulfill every dream I ever had. But then I'd have to set some new goals, and that's where the Dodger records come in."

Sutton was referring to lifetime Dodger records, many of which are held by another pitcher who labored for years in a Dodger uniform, Don Drysdale. By the conclusion of the 1979 season Sutton should possess club records in career wins, strikeouts, and shutouts.

The talented Sutton is also interested in broadcasting and has taken part in such off-the-field activities as announcing a Little League World Series game to a national television audience. Since his decision to trust in his Father completely, Sutton has experienced a great deal of joy and knows that he will always be enthusiastic about life.

"I'll always be a little kid. When I quit being a little kid, then I hope somebody will rap me on the noggin. It's Biblical that in order to be Christians we have to become as little children. I think in order to really enjoy life we have to have a little bit of a little kid in us. If you look at little children, they're unaffected, unassuming, they don't hold grudges, and they accept everything as though it was bright and new. Their approach to life is very refreshing. Simple things are big, and they appreciate simple things. They recuperate fast; a little rest and a kid's ready to go again."

Although Sutton realizes that adults have a responsibility to guide children, he feels that older people can learn much about life and God through children.

"They have no hangups, and that, to me, is so important. I think we older folks look at the world through distorted glasses, and live life through distorted views and viewpoints. I think that there's a lot we can learn from little children if we just leave them alone and let them teach us."

In Sutton's eyes a problem Christian children may encounter is the fear that classmates or friends may not fully accept them.

"I think probably the biggest hindrance to children or youngsters becoming Christian or living a Christian life is peer pressure, social pressure, pressure from the people around them, who will think that they are strange and different because they want to do that. But God really did tell us that we are supposed to be different. Instead of making it more difficult to live, becoming Christian gives us a better guideline and puts us on the right path. If we are Christians, we can understand if we're criticized and misunderstood. It makes living life a little easier."

Sutton has experienced the feeling of being gently lifted to his feet and strengthend by Jesus after a painful fall. During the waning weeks of the 1978 baseball season, newspapers and radio and television announcers across the country carried the jolting account of a clubhouse scuffle between Sutton and his popular teammate Steve Garvey. The disagreement surfaced in the Dodger clubhouse prior to a game with the Mets on a Sunday afternoon in New York. Garvey, apparently angered by some remarks concerning him made by Sutton in an interview with the Washington Post, confronted the Dodger hurler at his locker. The players talked for a brief time, but suddenly were locked together, rolling about on the floor. Sutton and Garvey were pulled apart by concerned teammates, and throughout the following days little more was heard concerning the situation.

On Thursday of that week Sutton, battling tears, read from a prepared statement before an audience of newspaper, radio, and televison reporters which had surrounded his locker at Dodger Stadium. Indicating first that he wished to "clear the air," Sutton went on:

"I thank God for Steve Garvey and for the role God has let him play in my life, and now I can thank God for the Washington Post article and for the disagreement in New York. .. together they have helped to point out to me very vividly that as long as my life isn't right, then I can't be a good example to anyone."

Sutton, explaining that the incident had dominated his thoughts for several days, added: "I've tried to figure out why this all had to happen, and the only possible reason I can find is that my life isn't being lived according to what I know as a human being and a Christian to be right, because if it were, then there would not have been an article in a newspaper in which I would offend any of my teammates."

"My role as a Christian," continued Sutton, "is to, at all costs, soothe those who are hurt and to prevent arguments. I could have done all that very easily with just the right word or explanation or apology. I humbly and sincerly apologize to anyone who has been embarrassed by this whole incident."

Living through such experiences as these has caused Sutton to realize that Jesus Christ stands kindly and patiently by his side, through storms as well as sunshine.

Don Sutton knows that no matter what he may do, Jesus Christ will always be present to forgive and comfort him.

"I'm really, really, very happy that I have Christ as a good Friend day after day after day," explained Sutton eagerly. "A good friend is someone who not only likes you when it's easy to be liked, but loves you when it's not so easy to love you and forgives you when you do things that they don't approve of. I'm not proud of it when I do those things, but I think the knowledge that Christ forgives me helps me to forgive myself.

"I'm my own worst critic. I expect more out of me than anybody else does. Christ is a forgiving Friend. He helps me get along with me. I've always been able to handle getting along with everybody else, but He helps me get along with me."

Look at the birds of the air: they neither sow nor reap nor gather into barns, and yet your heavenly Father feeds them. Are you not of more value than they?

Matthew 6:26 RSV

Chris Speier

Shortstop—Montreal Expos

With his heart fluttering beneath his crisp San Francisco Giants uniform, young Chris Speier slowly drew in a breath of the clean spring air. He ran his spikes gently through the fine dirt at the shortstop position, straightened his cap, then ventured a glance around vast San Diego Stadium, whose stands held an ocean of fans. After rifling a final warmup throw across the diamond, Speier eased back into his shortstop position, watching the first San Diego batter step into the batter's box. The visiting Giants were opening their 1971 season, and their newly-groomed shortstop, fresh from the minor leagues, was launching his major league career.

"Here I was, 20 years old, in my first year," reflected Speier. "I had been born and raised in San Francisco, and I had been somewhat of a Giants fan. I get out there in my first game and I look behind me and there's Willie Mays in center field, Willie McCovey on first base, and Juan Marichal on the mound. I was just in awe for about 5 or 10 minutes. It really hit me. I think that was one of the biggest thrills I've ever had."

On that April evening in San Diego, Chris Speier became the regular shortstop for the San Francisco Giants. Speier became a key ingredient on a club in the midst of a sizzling National League West Division title race. On the final day of that season Speier experienced another exhilarating moment.

"We won our division on the last day," he explained. "I made the final out to cap our victory; I caught the last ground ball of the game to send us into the playoffs against the Pittsburgh Pirates. That whole year was a tremendous time in my life, as far as baseball is concerned."

Throughout the following years, Speier's sparkling play earned for him a reputation as one of the game's most talented young players. In 1972, 1973, and 1974 the Giant infielder was named to National League All-Star squads, and in 1973 the Associated Press tabbed him the major league shortstop of the year. Speier remained with the San Francisco organization until the 1978 campaign, when he became a member of the Montreal Expos. His presence in the Montreal infield was one of the factors which enabled the Expos to become serious National League East contenders for the first time since the club's birth in 1969.

Chris Speier was brought up in the San Francisco area, and his life centered around sports, leaving little room for anything else.

"During my childhood, high school, and college years, God was never a part of my life," explained the lean infielder. "I didn't have time for Him. Other things were more important in my life; baseball and athletics were number one, along with an academic education to get to a college to play either baseball or basketball."

Speier's athletic dreams were soon realized, as he was selected in 1970 as the Giants' number one draft pick. He signed with the hometown club, and after a single campaign in the minor leagues, was called up to the majors. Though barely out of his teenage years, Speier came roaring into the big leagues, bold and brash. The young Californian was unintimidated by the seasoned talent which abounds in the National League and took little time in establishing himself there.

At 20 years of age, Chris Speier had become a regular on his hometown club, helping to spark it to a divisional championship. Despite all of this, the Giant newcomer felt himself groping for something more. His wife Aleta seemed to possess a deeper peace in her life, and Chris, realizing that something in his life had remained empty, began to hunger for it as well.

"When I was 21 or so, I met my wife, who is indeed the influence that made me make up my mind exactly how important God is and what kind of role He should play in our lives. It was through her faith and how she presented herself to me that I really saw where I had gone wrong. I saw a lot of things I had to do to change my life. It was the way she behaved, her example, that made me realize that 'Hey, I have a lot to be thankful for and there's a lot more that I can do as a person to grow.' It was through my wife that I finally saw, 'Hey, there's a Father who does care about us.'"

After he had made this commitment to the Lord, Speier began to ponder the idea of becoming a member of his wife's church. After much thought, he made the move, joining the Catholic Church. As the Holy Spirit began to flow into all areas of his being, Speier felt himself gradually being softened and transformed.

"I used to be quite a wild man," he admitted. "I learned through turning to Christ that you can handle your hostilities and aggression in other ways. I just found myself coming closer and closer to Christ. I learned to be a lot more sympathetic and understanding of and a little bit more patient with people and I see them in a different light."

Through coming to know how deeply God cares for every person, Speier began to reflect this kindness and goodness to those around him.

"God loves us all," he explained. "We don't have to agree with someone's actions, but we should love him as a person."

With this newly found attitude working in his life, Speier found that some of those around him felt that the change could hamper his baseball career.

"I had been a very aggressive and very hot-tempered young man," he explained, "and when I first turned to Christ, a lot of people felt that it hurt my career, because I had mellowed out, and they thought I was a little bit too lackadaisical."

It wasn't as if Speier no longer felt emotions such as anger; he was simply learning through Christ to channel them in directions which would no longer bring harm to himself and others.

"I think you have to realize that people have a lot of different personalities, and some people can keep their emotions inside of them and restrain them. The more I do that, the more it bothers me. I have to get them out. I've just learned that I can deal with them without having a lot of people see me."

Far from hindering his career, Speier's new friendship with Jesus filled him with zeal and zest.

"God didn't cause my playing career to go downhill; in fact, it's definitely helped me, because it's given me an incentive on a daily basis. I am very thankful to be able to go out there every day because I have God-given ability. To play each game for our Lord is incentive enough, and that is what I try to do."

Because the Holy Spirit is alive in his life, Speier finds that good works flow much more naturally from him than before.

"It's just like any other kind of relationship," said the All-Star infielder. "If you want to make your wife happy, you are going to try to do the things in your life that will make her happy. You grow by not wanting to do the things in your life that will take you away from Jesus, just because you love Him so much. You just find that the more that you keep in constant relationship with Him, the less you are going to do the things that make Him unhappy."

Yet, emphasized Speier, a Christian should not become impatient with himself for failing to love others and God perfectly; we will all slip frequently until we are completely one with the Father.

"It's a simple formula, but it's a difficult world to live in," admitted Speier. "This is what is so beautiful about our Father. He's such a forgiving Father. It's very difficult to live in society today and to really stay close with God because of the temptations, the evils which are present. It's good to know that when you do mess up, there is Someone who died for our sins, who really loves us a lot and is ready to take us back under His wing again."

What many baseball fans, especially children, do not understand at times, pointed out Speier, is the fact that their heroes, like all people, have flaws and weaknesses.

"No matter what, when you have an idol and that idol does not live up to your expectations, which he is not going to be able to do, you're always a little bit disappointed. But I think that kids should realize that major-leaguers are human beings, and we're all fallible and we all have faults. There was only one Person who was ever perfect, and they crucified Him."

Yet, although we as children of God are not yet completely like Him, through conversing with Him and sitting at His feet we can blossom into saints.

"I like the idea of being alone and really making Him present at any time," explained Speier. "It could be driving a car, a walk to the ball park from the hotel, or reading the Scriptures and listening to and comprehending His words.

"I think prayer is definitely important," he declared, adding that by keeping his door open, a Christian can usher God's light into a dim world.

"People would find that a lot of our problems on earth would be solved, I think."

Besides praying for situations in today's world which are tangled and need God's touch, Speier and his wife actively act as instruments to spread His goodness. On a special night in San Francisco in the early seventies their lives took a turn down this path.

"We were invited to a banquet in San Francisco, and the president of the National Right to Life group, Mildred Jefferson, was the head speaker there. We really did not know what to expect and had no idea what our commitment to Pro-Life would be, but we heard her speak and we were just totally amazed at what she said and what was going on. The more we got educated about abortion in the United States and around the world, the more we really wanted to help."

Since that night in San Francisco, the Speiers have devoted themselves intensely to attempting to halt legalized abortion and establish a respect for human life at all stages. Chris has had the opportunity to appear on television and radio and express his belief that abortion is the taking of an innocent human life. He has also formed a group known as "Athletes for Life," which is made up of other major league players such as Sal Bando and Joe Rudi.

"It will work in conjunction with the National Right to Life," explained Speier, referring to the nation's parent Pro-Life organization. "The players would make a commitment, like the people who fight multiple sclerosis. We want to go to basketball and football, just everything. I would be known as 'Chris Speier, an athlete for life who believes in life from the beginning of conception until natural end.'"

"What we want to do," continued Speier, "is to pass a constitutional amendment. That's the only way we can change what's going on in our society today. The only way we can pass a constitutional amendment is to get Pro-Life people in office, so if athletes would stand up for their convictions and stand behind a politician both financially and verbally, then I think that would help the candidate achieve office. What I really believe is that if a candidate doesn't respect life, I don't want to see any of the other issues. I think you have to begin there."

Speier has taken the bold move of speaking about the Pro-Life issue to as many major league teams as possible. When he is finished presenting the facts on the issue, he circulates response cards throughout his audience.

"They each give me a yes or no on how they feel about this Pro-Life business."

Those players responding with a yes will have an opportunity to become a member of "Athletes for Life" and to work for the cause of the organization.

Although Speier is a professional athlete, he considers himself first of all a servant of God, and thus is concerned about such off-the-diamond issues.

"I want to be respected as a baseball player, but I also want to be respected as a person."

Despite the overwhelming abundance of gifts which pour into the life of a child of God, any of those whose doors remain closed to Jesus explain their resistance by maintaining that to live for Him would be to surrender all that is enjoyable and live a dull life.

"It depends on what they mean by fun," responded Speier. "I am sure that they're thinking of some of the things that have really, I think, depleted society, but that's the lack of any kind of morals in our society today. To live a Christian life is not to go around being in reverent prayer for 24 hours a day. I have fun playing baseball, and I enjoy it. There are a lot of things that young people can do that I am sure would be enjoyable. It's just a matter of their commitment to God and how much they really love Him and stick by His Commandments."

If Jesus is the most important Person in our lives, added Speier, everything else will follow naturally and fall gently into place.

"If you continue to put your Father number one, everything else has a way of working itself out. It's funny, the more we get our priorities messed up and forget and drop Jesus to number two or three, the harder it becomes."

Realizing that his relationship with God is the most important part of his life, Speier frequently attends his club's Baseball Chapel services, soaking in the stories of how others, including many professional athletes, have discovered Jesus' love in their lives.

"I think more and more players are being open about their Christian lives. At times you are put into situations where you have the opportunity to speak about Jesus, and one of these times is during our Sunday chapel programs. Now I think it's a subject that you can freely discuss, where before it was something that a lot of people felt a little bit hindered or questioning about. I don't want to push it down anybody's throat, but if I have the opportunity to speak about our Lord, I will."

In fact, Chris Speier's most satisfying moments in baseball have come, not from stealing a key base or diving for a screaming line drive, but from working in his Lord's garden.

"I can't remember, say, a big home run or a game-winning hit or something like that, but I think one thrill has been the response of the guys on this Right-to-Life message that I have; a lot of them are taking some interest and seem to really be giving me some encouragement or saying, 'That's really a good thing you are doing.' And this is just giving me a lot of satisfaction."

Another source of happiness and fulfillment in Speier's life is his family; he and his wife have three children—Justin, Erika, and Luke.

The story of Chris Speier is a clear example of God's love entering a heart. Although he had experienced a good deal of success early in his career, he was thirsting for something deeper. He found that Jesus Christ was seeking to give him life in its fullness, and by receiving that gift, has found a new and fulfilling joy.

"There's been a tremendous change, and I am sure that it's been a change for the better," reflected the quiet infielder. "I know I am a much happier person than I was six or seven years ago. It's so much easier to have a clear picture of where you are going if you keep God number one in your life."

> For we know that if the earthly tent we live in is destroyed, we have a building from God, a house not made with hands, eternal in the heavens.
>
> 2 Corinthians 5:1 RSV

Gary Lavelle

Pitcher—San Francisco Giants

Carefully easing out of his black and orange warmup jacket, Gary Lavelle came to his feet in the National League bullpen. Reaching for his glove, the San Francisco relief pitcher let his eyes sweep through the colorful stands of Yankee Stadium, filled completely on this evening for the 1976 major league All-Star game. Lavelle sent his fingers deep into his glove, then embarked upon the long journey to the vacant pitcher's mound. He slowly crossed the white chalk of the foul line and then the neatly trimmed grass of the field. Arriving at the mound, he reached for the ball resting near it, then straightened, climbed the dirt hill, and began to smooth it with his spikes. Within moments the San Francisco pitcher was sending baseballs hissing into the mitt of catcher Ted Simmons.

The National League had erupted early in the midsummer classic and now in the last half of the fourth inning held a 5-0 edge.

89

The American League, however, featured an awesome array of hitters; and thus no opposing pitcher, despite even a lead of several runs, could feel completely comfortable.

The first American League batter, George Brett, soon planted his spikes into the carefully raked dirt of the batter's box and slowly waved the wood in his strong hands. Lavelle gazed in past the young Kansas City third baseman, then went into his windup and delivered.

Brett's taut stance vanished as he stepped forward, the bat whipping in an arc past the blue Royals emblem on his chest. There was a muffled crack, and the ball soared lazily into left field, where San Diego's Dave Winfield circled briefly before gathering it in.

The next A.L. All-Star was Carl Yastrzemski, in the twilight of a brilliant career with the Boston Red Sox. The San Francisco standout whiffed the Hall-of-Fame bound Yaz, and, after permitting a single to Richie Zisk, fanned celebrity Yankee outfielder Reggie Jackson. By the time Lavelle had returned to the cool of the dugout, he had faced four of the American League's most talented hitters, holding them scoreless. In the fifth inning, the All-Star left-hander again took the mound, successfully retiring Carlton Fisk, Rick Burleson, and Larry Hisle on routine plays. Though a newcomer to the All-Star contest, Lavelle had demonstrated quite clearly the reason for his budding reputation as one of baseball's most reliable relief artists.

It was only a few seasons earlier, however, that Lavelle had seriously wondered if he ever again would stand atop a pitcher's mound and compete professionally. Though a member of the San Francisco organization since his teens, Lavelle had remained in the minor leagues well into his twenties, and began to fear that a genuine chance at the big leagues would never come about and that he would thus have to abandon the game to which he had been dedicated since early childhood.

Gary Lavelle was born in Scranton, Pennsylvania, the youngest of five boys. Early in Gary's life, the Lavelles moved to Bethlehem,

Pennsylvania, where he spent his boyhood years romping with his brothers.

"My four older brothers were always into sports," he explained. "I can remember always going out after school and playing sports, you know, baseball, basketball, and football, the three main sports. I used to enjoy playing all of them. I started pitching in Little League, and I've always enjoyed pitching, but I really never considered pitching as a career by any means."

By the time he reached high school, however, the youngest Lavelle had come to regard his fondness for baseball as something which could one day flourish into a career.

"I don't think it was until high school that I really made up my mind to be a good pitcher or felt that pitching could be my career," revealed Lavelle. "I remember in ninth grade the guidance counselor asked us what we wanted to be and what we'd like to do, and I put down playing baseball."

A year later Lavelle experienced a thrilling moment on the high school diamond and as a result his confidence began to increase.

"I threw a no-hitter in 10th grade," he recalled with satisfaction. "I really enjoyed pitching after that. I felt I was starting to expand in my ability as a pitcher. In 11th grade I started getting letters from various teams and was invited to summer tryout camps. It was my best year in high school, and a lot of scouts were really starting to become interested in me."

Although Lavelle's senior season was clouded by a rather severe case of tendonitis, one of his deepest and most precious dreams was fulfilled during that year.

"Even though I pitched most of the year with a sore arm, we won our district and I was drafted by the Giants. It was really a shock. I remember the morning before our district championship I got a phone call, never thinking that it could be a scout telling me that I would be drafted, but it was. It seemed like the happiest moment of my life at that time, because as a child I had always loved the Giants, I had always wanted to play major league baseball, and with the Giants. The Giants were my favorite team, so it all fit in really well. And it was like a dream come true as far as being able to at least say that I signed with the Giants."

Lavelle was assigned to a minor league club, and spent the next eight seasons hurling at various levels of the San Francisco organization, performing with determination, but still receiving no invitation to make the trip to the majors.

"I was really struggling," reflected Lavelle of his years on the Giant farm clubs. "I had control problems. I felt at times I should have been up, but I never got the shot."

In 1974 Lavelle played his third season at Phoenix, a Triple-A team and the final step before the majors. The quiet athlete was nearing his midtwenties and yet could see no light on the horizon. A brilliant spring on the mound and a shortage of Giant southpaws, however, were enough for Lavelle to remain hopeful that this season would be different than those in the past.

"I really got off to a good start," explained Lavelle of the 1974 season at Phoenix. "It just seemed like the Giants didn't have any left-handed pitching. I was anxious; I felt that they were going to call me up because I was the last one cut from the roster that year during spring training. I really felt that they'd give me a shot."

Lavelle believed that he had reached the end of a long and rugged path; he felt as if he were about to step out of the forest of minor league obscurity into the sunlight of the big leagues. Already daring to envision himself in a Giants uniform, Lavelle continued to hurl steadily and effectively. The middle of the season arrived, and with it a chance to build upon the splendid beginning which he had enjoyed, and thus attract the attention of the San Francisco club. Suddenly, however, Lavelle's winning pattern disrupted, and with it all apparent hope of being promoted to the big club.

"I just started going downhill," recounted Lavelle. 'It hit me like a thunderbolt. 'This is it,' I thought, 'I'll never get my shot.' I lost five or six games in a row; everything started going haywire. I was really depressed and thinking about retiring from baseball."

Knocked to the earth and stunned by what was taking place,

Lavelle groped feebly for something to steady him, for it appeared as if he had arrived at a cruel dead end.

"I got hold of a book of prayers. I just took it along. I just kept praying each and every day, reaching out. I guess at that time it was desperation, because baseball had been my life, and I felt I really couldn't be happy unless I had made the major leagues and fulfilled that dream that I've always had. I didn't even really know if there was a God at this time, because I had gotten away from church; I had gotten away from whatever I had ever felt about the Lord."

Bewildered by the course his life was taking, Lavelle longed for something to soothe the pain and uncertainty cutting into his heart.

"I was searching, I was really searching," said Lavelle emphatically. "I had no idea what a relationship with Christ was, but it was through this that I reached out. I felt that, 'If there is a God there, I hope You would answer me.'"

The season dwindled to a close, and Lavelle began to pack his glove and spikes and shuffle away for another long off-season.

"It was at this time that our manager came up to me and said, 'You're going up to the big leagues,' probably the most unlikely thing I ever thought he would say. It was after I ended up 8-14. I had just had a horrible year, and that was the least thing I expected.

"Evidently, they were going to see if I could pitch up there or release me," Lavelle continued. "I was thinking about retiring at that time. I got called up to the big leagues, and in my mind it was the happiest day of my life."

Lavelle became a member of the San Francisco bullpen, and despite an 0-3 showing, performed well throughout the remainder of the summer. After this brief experience as a major-leaguer, he began to feel an inner certainty that he could pitch successfully at that level.

"I really felt that I could pitch in the major leagues, and the Giants were going to give me a shot. At that time my dream was realized; I finally made the major leagues and fulfilled that dream that I had always had. I had never had the opportunity; you always doubt yourself unless you get the chance to prove it."

Lavelle was overjoyed; he had arrived at the top rung of professional baseball's ladder. Yet, as the months passed and he began to blend into the Giant pitching staff, the glow and newness of major league baseball began to fade.

"At that time, I realized that there was something missing, you know. It really didn't satisfy me because I knew that someday this world would come to a halt."

Thus Gary Lavelle, after weathering almost a decade in the minor leagues, had risen into the glamorous world of the major leagues, only to be startled by the discovery that his heart was still tossing restlessly.

"I just started questioning what life is all about, and for two years I kept asking those questions. I began reading the Bible. I really coudn't comprehend anything at that time."

During the course of the 1975 season, his first full major league campaign, Lavelle occasionally attended the team's Sunday morning chapel services, but was not completely able to understand all that was being said about Christ.

I kept listening to these Christian speakers. They go through the prayer of salvation once in a while, and I said it, but I really didn't realize what I was doing or what I was saying. I felt I was getting closer; I was trying to grasp onto something to see what truth is and what life is all about."

The season came to its autumn close with Lavelle still thirsting inwardly, and it was in this state that the Giant moundsman encountered a fellow hurler whose own flame of love for Jesus brought a new spark into Lavelle's heart.

"After the season I went to Venezuela, and I met this beautiful brother in the Lord, Tom Johnson, a pitcher for the Minnesota Twins. Tom shared with me about the relationship he had with Jesus Christ. We talked hours about it; he answered all the questions I had. I know the Lord put him there for a purpose, and I guess I was his purpose; the Lord brought him my way.

94

"One night in November I just got down on my knees and asked the Lord to come into my life, and He did. The next morning I told Tom what I did, and I was baptized in this big swimming pool down there at the hotel, and my walk with God started then."

As soon as he yielded his heart to Jesus Christ, the scattered pieces of his life began to gradually come together.

"I just felt a peace when I did that; a peace that I couldn't really explain, but it was the most peaceful thing I've ever felt in my whole life. I just knew that this was what I had been searching for."

Soon after this time, Lavelle encountered some Christian friends who, at his request, gathered around him and prayed for a deeper and fuller release of the Holy Spirit already within him. Following this "baptism" in the Spirit, Lavelle drew even closer to God, and was thus filled with a new power to love.

"It opened up a new dimension of my spiritual growth," said Lavelle simply. "Of course, we have our trials and struggles, but I know the Lord is living in me, and I've been growing tremendously since that time.

"All our lives we exercise our bodies and our minds, but we do very little spiritual exercising. I try to put that into perspective, that the most important thing in my life now is to exercise my spirit, that I might become the complete man the Lord talks about in the Bible.

"In the past several years my priorities have totally turned around," he continued. "I put Jesus first and everything else second. At times we struggle and we don't give the Lord all our worries and pressures; or if a problem comes up, we try to solve it ourselves, and we always seem to be failing. All the time the Lord is still there saying, 'Why don't you give it to Me; I'll take care of it for you.'"

One explanation for the tendency which Christians have for clinging to their own difficulties and painful situations is that they lack trust in God.

"Our views of God's love for us are distorted, I believe, because we think the love He has for us is the type of love we have for others; because when someone does something wrong to us, we sometimes like to get back at them. I think we have that same feeling when we mess up in our walk with Him, that the Lord is always trying to get back at us. That's not the case at all. I think Satan would have you believe that, but of course it isn't true. He loves us all the time, the same way all the time."

Knowing God's affection for him more intimately each day, Lavelle feels an increasing enthusiasm about all of life. Some people, however, think that surrendering themselves to God would force them to give up all which they enjoy.

"No, not at all," exclaimed Lavelle. "My walk has been exciting, even though at times I've stumbled and fallen. He is always there to pick me up and to lead me onto a higher level so that I can grow more each and every day with Him. It's just tremendous."

The dark-haired hurler went on to express his joy in knowing a Lord whose love for him is so real and complete.

"Jesus is there to accept you no matter who you are. He will receive all who come to Him. I think this is especially important for youngsters in this day and age who are seeking something that will give them peace or fulfillment in their lives. The young people nowadays seem to be definitely searching more than before, but they're always looking for something that is going to be a false fulfillment. Since some people look up to athletes, I think it's so important to be able to tell them about what Jesus Christ has done in your life."

Thus, when Lavelle is not playing baseball or at home with his wife Regina and daughter Jana Marie, he spends time speaking before young people, expressing the contentment he experiences in his friendship with Christ, as well as discussing baseball with them. Children today are exposed to a wide spectrum of philosophies and beliefs, and Lavelle hopes to warn them away from any which might confuse them or keep them from coming into the arms of Jesus.

"You can see the movements going on now in the United States," cautioned Lavelle. "There are different Eastern religions, such as Transcendental Meditation. These groups come on and say, 'We'll teach you a new way to relax and to be happy.' And it's causing people to worship an idol. There are so many people being deceived. I think it's important for us as Christians to stand up and start speaking out on a lot of things going on in this country. There have been a lot of false religions going around. It's time that people know that that's not worshiping the true God. I feel it's up to the Christians, because no one else is going to do it."

Because of all the gifts which the Father has lavished upon him, the Giant bullpen specialist eagerly wishes to serve Him by spreading the Good News to those around him, including other big-leaguers.

"I feel it's important for me as a player to be open to witnessing to the other players. I witness a lot on a one-to-one basis. I don't push anybody. I feel that if they want to ask me some questions, I'm always here to answer them if I can. I believe the Lord has put me on this team for that reason, and it's really enjoyable to see other guys come to the Lord; it's such a fulfillment within myself. It's hard to describe. It's a joy because I realize how much it's changed my life, and it's enjoyable to see somebody else come to the Lord. He'll help them grow and they'll live a better life. The Lord says that our most important witness is our actions. Hopefully, most of the guys know how I feel about Jesus Christ, how much I love the Lord and try to live the best life I can. I'm not saying that I live a perfect life by any means, but I try to be a witness for the other guys."

Lavelle realizes that Christians, though weak in themselves, carry the glory of God within them, and can allow the pure light of His forgiveness and love to shine into a darkened world.

"He said not to hide the lights He's given us. I shines a lot more up on a hill than hiding in a closet. I feel that a lot of Christians have been hiding in the closet and not speaking out on their faith, and I think the Lord wants us to speak out on our faith. Not in a pushy way, but in a way that people know where we stand."

It is clear, then, that the life of Gary Lavelle, once broken, has been refashioned by the gentle hands of his Father, and continues toward wholeness each day. Lavelle's baseball career, once drifting without meaning, has become a window through which the goodness of God can warm a cool world.

"There's been a noticeable change in my life, for sure," he marvelled. "Before I came to know the Lord, I was very much a pessimistic person, usually about my ability. Coming to know Christ was the most important thing I've ever done.

"There's excitement and growth in the walk with Jesus. To know God is a great and exciting experience. I want people to know that Christianity is not a religion at all, but a relationship with Jesus Christ."

See! (said the Lord Jesus), I stand at the door and knock. When anyone hears My voice and opens the door, I will come in to him, and we will eat together.

Revelation 3:20
The Holy Bible for Children
© CPH 1977

Pat Kelly

Outfielder—Baltimore Orioles

His arms and legs leaping to life, Pat Kelly broke into a steady run. Gathering speed, the Baltimore Oriole outfielder swept ahead, a grin on his face. His graceful and powerful strides became longer, and he soon was gliding swiftly past those around him.

Kelly was not in the midst of chasing a long drive to left field or trying to stretch a double into a triple, he was hurrying down the busy streets of Baltimore.

"Sometimes I'll be running on the street; nobody's behind me, but I'm running. I feel so good sometimes, it scares me. That's God living in me. I know God lives today because He lives in me. I tried Him one day; that's why I know about Him.

"Every day is a joy!" he exclaimed. "Things that I couldn't cope with before—the anger, fear, and jealousy—have fled me. There's peace, there's love and giving. You cannot begin to live until you share the joy of God."

These are the words of Pat Kelly, a major league baseball player for more than a decade. Baseball has always been at the heart of Pat Kelly's life; until a special day in 1975 he lived for nothing else.

Kelly spent his childhood years in Philadelphia, Pennsylvania, where he played his favorite sport with all the intensity of a boy longing to someday play in the big leagues.

"All my life baseball was my one and only ambition," Kelly recalled. "It was just morning, noon, and night. To this day I accuse my dad of throwing a baseball into my crib. As far back as I can remember, that's all I ever wanted to do. Playing in the big leagues is a dream come true."

Pat, however, was not the only outstanding athlete to come from the Kelly family; his older brother, Leroy, went into professional football, starring for the Cleveland Browns for 10 years.

"I need not say where his talents have taken him," said Kelly proudly. "The guys on my team say, 'Well, you're just Leroy Kelly's little brother; he's the athlete in the family.' I love him dearly, and I enjoyed watching him run just as much as everybody else."

As he was growing up in Philadelphia, Kelly played in several baseball leagues. By the time he reached high school, his athletic skills were developed to the point that the coaches there pleaded with him to play other sports as well.

"I just wanted to play baseball, but the coaches said I had a family tradition to live up to. I was the last Kelly; three brothers had gone before me. They all played baseball, basketball, and football. I went out and did well in football and basketball, but when it was all over, baseball was the one thing I wanted to do."

Kelly's parents had to work extremely hard to support and care for their healthy and hungry sons, along with the other Kelly children.

"My father worked for $12 a week to serve nine kids and put food on our table. He would wake up at four in the morning and it would be freezing cold outside. He would go in a pickup truck with no heat some 30 miles and work all day, but he went with God in his heart."

On many summer evenings, as the Kellys settled down for their evening meal, young Pat could be found outside, feverishly working on his hitting or getting together one last neighborhood game before the sun sank away. Kelly said later that as a child he preferred baseball to eating.

Kelly entered high school, and his baseball ability immediately attracted much attention. In his freshman season he was already being watched closely by a major league scout. By the time he graduated, scouts and recruiters were banging on his door.

"When I came out of high school, I had the biggest decision of my life to make—either accept a college scholarship or an offer to play professional baseball."

After pondering the situation for a while, the young athlete reached a decision.

"After thinking it over for a long time, I couldn't see turning down the one thing I wanted all my life, to play professional baseball. In college I might have gotten hurt and never been able to do the one thing I wanted to do, so I signed, and I haven't regretted it to this day."

Kelly became a member of the Minnesota Twins organization and began a steady climb to the major leagues. His first chance to crack a big-league lineup came in 1969, with a new American League club, the Kansas City Royals, which came about through expansion. After two seasons as a Royal, Kelly was traded to another American League team, the Chicago White Sox. Kelly played for the Sox for the next six campaigns, and although he had launched his major league career in Kansas City, Chicago found a place in his heart.

"I came to love the city," he said. "The people really treated me wonderfully."

In 1976, following another trade, Kelly found himself playing in a Baltimore Orioles uniform, which he has worn throughout the latter years of the seventies.

103

It was during his time in Chicago that Kelly experienced his most thrilling moment as a major-leaguer.

"We were playing Milwaukee," recalled Kelly, "and it was a nationally televised game. I knew my parents and all my friends and buddies, everybody, was watching. Bill Travers, a left-hander from Milwaukee, was pitching. He kind of pitched around a couple of guys to get to me, and wound up loading the bases."

Kelly then stepped to the plate and belted a Travers delivery into the seats for his first major league grand-slam home run.

"That was truly the thrill of a lifetime," savored Kelly.

Despite such moments as these, the Pennsylvania native began to experience a restlessness and confusion during his final days in Chicago.

"I fell in love with a charming young lady in Chicago, and need not say what love can do to somebody. I was lost for identity; the Pat Kelly that I could relate to for thirty years I was no longer relating to. My mind and emotions were going through different changes. My nerves were on edge. I was torn and confused."

Up until this time in his life Kelly had prayed to God when he desperately needed something, but after receiving that which he had asked for, had gone on his way, forgetting about God until another emergency arose.

"As long as it was just my ankle, it was fine: Dear God, bless my ankle, let it get better. Dear God, bless my shoulder so that the operation will go fine and I can go on and play.' My mother would get sick: 'Dear God, bless my mother, let her get better.' She gets well, and I'm back on the streets, partying and doing my own thing, saying, 'Everything's fine, I don't need God anymore.' I'd call on Him only when I'd need Him."

But in 1975, while still playing in Chicago, Kelly began to realize that he was helpless to deal with the worries and pressures which were exhausting him. When his suffering reached a climax, Kelly decided that it was time to do something.

"I went to a friend of mine, a Christian man from Chicago, Mr. Clyde White. He's a bank executive. I was just going to cash a check, and I looked terrible—I had lost weight, I couldn't sleep, all the symptoms of someone deeply confused. I went to Clyde that day and said, 'Clyde, I don't know why, but I've got problems in my life. I've just come off a fine season, I've got some money in the bank, my folks are well; but I'm very confused. I need some help. I need some spiritual help.' And he called me into his office, and I cried out to him like a child."

White responded by asking Kelly to his home for a Bible study that evening. Kelly accepted his friend's invitation, and a few hours later found himself sitting among a group of warm, concerned people. After listening carefully to the Christians there and the words of the Bible, Kelly saw that his unhappiness and pain could be taken away by only one Person, Jesus Christ. On that night, the ballplayer from Philadelphia surrendered control of his life to the Lord, asking Him to take over a sinking ship.

From that evening on, God began to mend Kelly's life, gently placing the pieces together. Although Kelly would have liked for his problems to be erased magically, it was only through a daily process of openness to Jesus that a new peace and joy began to emerge.

"See, I wanted to take a pill and just have all my problems gone. But it doesn't work that way. I gave my life over to Christ; that's the beginning. It didn't all come at once, because at that time I still had reservations. I still had doubts. I didn't know what God had in store for me. God is the Potter, we are the clay. He is the only One who can take all the pieces and put them back together."

In the days and weeks which followed Kelly began to grow rapidly in his new life.

"I continued to pray, read the Bible, and seek His kingdom. I prayed, 'Father, give me understanding. Show me the way.'

"We've got two bodies, a physical body and a spiritual body. We give our physical body food to nourish it; we must feed our spiritual body. That's what I began to do."

Kelly emphasized that knowing facts about God is not

enough; we must come to know Him as a Friend in whom we place all our trust.

"We all know about God," explained Kelly. "We've gone to church. We've gone to Sunday school. But see, there comes a time in everybody's life when he has to make that all-important decision. In Revelation 3:20 it states, 'Behold, I am constantly knocking at the door of your heart.' I thank God today because He enabled me to hear the knock at the door. For thirty years I had thought I knew Him, but here was doubt."

The American league athlete was referring to his uncertainty as to whether when his life on earth had been concluded he would find himself in heaven with God.

"We had a guest speaker at our chapel service who mentioned how before he was converted, he would weigh the good and bad in himself. He knew he had some bad, but he thought he had more good than bad. I was the same way, and I figured that God would weigh all the good that I had and because of that I would go to heaven. But I still had doubts; I didn't really know."

Much to his joy, however, Kelly has begun to understand that God wants him in His home despite his flaws and weaknesses.

"Once you repent, all your sins are washed away," he said. "You are a new creature; all things become new. You're cleansed."

Yet, coming in sorrow to the feet of Jesus is only the dawn of a new life; it naturally takes time for all of the darkness to give way to light.

"It doesn't make me perfect," stressed Kelly. "I don't claim to be perfect. That's the only thing I regret—that I cannot be perfect like my Savior."

Yet, a Christian can blossom more fully every day through the touch of the Holy Spirit, who lives within his heart.

"Jesus told His disciples in the book of John, 'I am telling you these things while I am here, but when I leave, My Father shall send the Holy Spirit, the Comforter.' The Holy Spirit gets us over our everyday lives, our everyday trials and tribulations. Maybe tomorrow I might have a problem, but I don't care. I know I've got my Lord."

Because of God's presence, Kelly does not become deeply discouraged with himself if he stumbles on the path.

"Satan's biggest control over us is that he makes us feel guilty. But hey! He can't make me feel guilty! I know why Jesus died on the cross. John 3:16 says, 'For God so loved the world that He gave His only begotten Son, so that whoever believes in Him shall not perish, but have everlasting life.'"

Thus Kelly is coming to know that God eagerly accepts him, looking upon him with love and compassion rather than with harshness.

"What did Jesus say to the people who wanted to stone the woman in the gospel? 'Let him who is without sin cast the first stone.' He's merciful. God loves you regardless of what you've been or done. Just repent of your sins and ask for forgiveness. The first step is to acknowledge that we as individuals are sinners and in need."

This magnificent love, added Kelly, is something which God longs to pour into every heart.

"As Jesus told the lady at the well, 'My well is a perpetuating well. You'll never thirst.'"

The sparkling river of God's forgiveness is always flowing freely; we need only to bend over and drink from it.

"Jesus is water in a dry land; He's bread in a starving land. Jesus is a friend when you don't have a friend. Prayer is a privilege. God's line is never busy. You might need a doctor and you call and he's not there, his line's busy. But with God, you can just get on your knees morning, noon, or night. I'm constantly praying; it's a way of life. God's just as real to me as a person sitting next to me, and until God becomes real like that in your own life, you don't know Him. You have to make that commitment."

The buoyant Kelly then expressed this idea through a story which he had heard from a minister.

"It's like the story of the chicken and the pig. The chicken told the pig, 'Let's serve these starving people.' And the pig said, 'What should we serve them?' So the chicken looked at the pig and said, 'Well, let's serve them ham and eggs.' The pig thought for a moment and he said, 'Well, that's fine for you to say; it's only a contribution for you, but for me it's a total commitment.' Until you make the total commitment to Christ, you can't really know Him.

"You can't serve God and have hatred in your heart; you can't serve God with jealousy and envy. No, you can't serve Him, because it's a barrier. When God takes up residence in your soul, Satan flees you; you can see through the trickery of Satan."

Any person can have a deep friendship with Christ, something which Kelly tries to get across to those to whom he speaks at various gatherings.

"I've spoken to kids; I've had an opportunity to go to a few churches and give testimonies. It's just a way of life with me now. I'll talk about baseball and then I can't help but go into speaking about Christ. People say, 'Well, Pat, it's easy for you to turn to God because you're a big-league ballplayer; you've got a car, you've got clothes, you've got money. Yes, I thank God for my baseball, for giving me the opportunity to play; but see, when you come to serve Him and know Him, you realize the little things we have to feel blessed about."

Kelly has enjoyed many such happy moments, such as the time before a game when a young boy gave Pat a gift—a Bible.

"This is the joy of serving God," beamed Kelly.

While speaking before groups, Kelly explains that God's gifts are available to all persons, from star athletes to those whose lives may seem unknown or unimportant.

"We all need God in our lives. Don't think anybody is without sin and problems.

"As athletes, we are looked up to, idolized, and admired by kids; but that's why we need to speak out for God, to let people know we're not athletes, but first of all servants of God."

Just as everyone endures suffering and loneliness of some kind, all people, regardless of race, age, or background, can come to know Jesus Christ and experience His cleansing and forgiving love.

"Salvation is so simple; all it is is repenting of your sin. People make it complex. The Bible says that the most intelligent individual will be made to seem stupid. We must humble ourselves as children. A lot of us have so much pride."

Kelly believes that God has placed him in the major leagues in order to spread the Good News, and that His Spirit works in a special way through each Christian.

"I enjoy witnessing and talking about God because I realize how wonderful and merciful He is. Witnessing doesn't mean that you have to go up and down the street hollering. God will place people in your path.

"This is how God is using me. He said some will be able to preach well, some will be able to heal, and some will just be able to be kind to people. We all have a part. Jesus said, 'Wear my yoke, for it fits perfectly around your neck.'"

Kelly eagerly works to build God's kingdom so that it might be whole and beautiful for the day when Jesus comes back for it.

"The day will come when He returns," said a smiling Kelly. "We will be transformed in the twinkling of an eye. There will be no more suffering, no more starving. I pray that God's kingdom will be on earth as it is in heaven. This is what faith is about, believing in something you have not already seen."

Thus Pat Kelly, whether roaming the outfield or standing before a crowd of youngsters, will spend the rest of his life on earth preparing for the day when he will join his Lord in heaven forever. Until then, Kelly and his wife Phyllis, whom he married in February of 1979, will continue to love their Lord.

"It's just a joy serving God," bubbled Kelly. "It's a peace, a serenity. It's a beauty beyond man's imagination. I don't want to do anything the rest of my life except to serve Him, put Him before everything.

"My treasures and rewards are in heaven with the Father," he went on. "This is not our home. We'll put on our white robes and walk all over God's heaven and just praise His holy name. There will be no more waking up at three in the morning with tears and loneliness. Oh, it's going to be a glorious day!

"I thank Him because I'm not stumbling, I'm walking in the light of God. I don't claim to be perfect but see, I know of an old Pat Kelly, and I know of a new one."

In My Father's house are many rooms; if it were not so, would I have told you that I go to prepare a place for you? And when I go and prepare a place for you, I will come again and will take you to Myself, that where I am you may be also.

John 14:2-3 RSV

Don Kessinger

Second Baseman Player-Coach—Chicago White Sox

Dusk was settling in over Chicago, and the August sun was slipping away beyond the walls of Comiskey Park, home of the city's American League baseball team, the White Sox. As the shadows on the field lengthened, the stadium's lights began to flicker on, revealing a restless and murmuring crowd of 45,000 fans.

All summer long the White Sox had been entangled in one of the most thrilling pennant races in its history, and throughout the exciting season, the fans of Chicago had come to know well the members of their home club. Yet, on this evening a new member of the team was present, a man who had spent 11 of his major league seasons laboring for the crosstown Chicago Cubs, Don Kessinger. The veteran switch-hitter had recently come to the Sox in a trade with the St. Louis Cardinals.

"I had no idea what the reception would be," Kessinger would recall later of his return to the Windy City.

Kessinger was not listed on the game's starting lineup card, and thus watched the contest from the cool darkness of the dugout. The White Sox were hosting the explosive New York Yankees, and by the seventh inning the visitors led 3-0. In the last half of the inning Chicago's Lamar Johnson doubled in two runs, and manager Bob Lemon looked down the bench at Kessinger and told him to pinch-run for Johnson. The slender newcomer climbed the steps of the dugout and bounded out onto the brilliant green of the field.

The packed stands of Comiskey Park began to rustle. A roar steadily arose, growing and swelling as it swept across the stadium, finally flooding forth into a thunder of cheering voices and a sea of colors as every person in the stadium came to his feet to greet Don Kessinger.

"It was really pleasing to me," reflected Kessinger of the response. "It really meant a great deal to me under the circumstances for them to give to me what represented a welcome home. They treated me like a king. It really meant a lot to me.".

In the eighth inning Kessinger's first turn at bat arrived. As he emerged from the dugout, another standing ovation rocked the rafters of the park.

These gestures of respect for Kessinger brought some brightness into the twilight of a relatively disappointing season, one which Kessinger had begun in a St. Louis Cardinal uniform. The durable second-sacker had been dispatched to the Cards prior to the 1975 season, and went on to play in nearly every game for the Redbirds that summer. When 1977 came around, however, the Cardinals were experiencing a trend toward youth, and Kessinger found himself spending more and more time on the bench. Finally, in late August, the seasoned shortstop was dealt to the White Sox.

Thus, considering the kind of season it had been, the reception which Kessinger received was especially meaingful to him. Yet, an even greater moment came forth a few weeks later, when the agile infielder was named the recipient of the first annual Danny

Thompson Memorial Award, an honor given to the player who "most exemplifies the Christian spirit throughout major league baseball." Kessinger had received other honors throughout his career; he was awarded two Gold Gloves and had been selected for the National League All-Star team on six occasions. Yet, the Danny Thompson Award came as an unexpected, yet thrilling event for him.

"I was very much surprised, and pleasantly, I might add," recounted Kessinger. "Considering that it was really a very long summer for me, it was ironic that I should receive what is probably the best award I've received."

Yet, those who know the steady shortstop by the award know that Kessinger has devoted himself to serving God since his youth.

Born in Forrest City, Arkansas, Kessinger grew up in a closely knit family which drew its life from God. Thus it is only natural that Kessinger has felt the companionship of Jesus Christ throughout his life.

"Fortunately, I was raised in a family in which we were in church twice on Sunday and once in the middle of the week, not because that's where you were supposed to be, but it was where my parents wanted to be. I was raised in a family which had prayer at mealtime. You realize that God is not someone you talk about for one hour on Sunday. Christ is in you all the time."

At age 12 the budding athlete opened himself to receive the presence of Jesus, allowing God to live within him and work in his life.

"Being raised in a Christian family is fine," he explained, "but you still have to make that commitment."

Since that time in his life, Kessinger has felt the gentle hand of Christ lifting and supporting him, even in his weakness.

"The Lord has been with me all the way," he maintained. "I don't know of anything outwardly different that anybody could tell you; I don't know of anything I could put my finger on except I know I was a very happy young man. I certainly felt no better than anybody else. I know I have my own hangups and I make my own mistakes. I just know that I have the assurance the Lord has the power to forgive them.

"All I know is that all the way up everybody has been exceptionally nice to me, and I've never had any problem getting along with people. I trust in people. I have a lot of faith in people. Very few times has that faith been unjustified. Someone has to really prove to me they're not worthy of my trust."

Kessinger went on to explain what being a Christian means to him.

"The heart of Christianity, to me, is very simply Jesus Christ. I know that because He died on the cross for me, I have the assurance that I can go to heaven. I know that He rose on the third day and conquered death. If Jesus Christ wasn't able to conquer death, then He couldn't save me from my sins; and I believe that He did, and that's the central theme of my faith."

Thus Kessinger places God above everything else in his life.

"I think that Christ is the center of Christianity, there's just no other way. You have to put Christ first in your life over all things. I think my priorities are Christ first, my family second, and my profession third. I believe that's the way it should be. If you keep Christ first in your life, then everything else tends to fall into place."

Kessinger admitted that he is unable to describe this tranquility; he only knows that it is a gift from God.

"The Bible describes it as a peace that passeth all understanding, and unless you've experienced that peace, you don't understand it; I just know there's a great assurance in it. It's just something that's inside you. You know you have a loving God who lives within you and has the power to forgive you. He understands you, He wants you just like you are, and you don't have to try to be someone else. He made you, and he never made a mistake, so He must have made you just like He wanted you to be. And so you have to accept that. It's just a great peace, but unless you appreciate and accept that, you can't understand that peace."

Kessinger realizes that Jesus can use him as an instrument to extend this peace and serenity to others.

"I believe that you live a lot better sermon than you preach, particularly when you're not in the ministry, you're in the business world; and that's what we're in. It's a little more in the public eye, but it's still a job. I believe by the life you live, people will know. They may not know what it is, but they'll know something is different about you. They'll know you have a peace which they don't have, and things seem to be a little more level for you and not so many peaks and valleys.

"I never try to condemn anyone; I don't believe in that at all. I never try to judge anyone else. I believe that there's a personal relationship between a man and his Lord."

Yet, Kessinger has experienced occasional opportunities to express to others how wonderfully God has worked in his life.

"If you try to live the way that you know is right, many times people will question you about that or ask you to share with them what you believe. And also the fact that the Baseball Chapel program has grown to such an extent gives me an opportunity to answer a lot of questions for people and share what Christ means to me."

Before the Baseball Chapel program developed to where it is today, however, Kessinger and some Chicago Cub teammates were coming together regularly for prayer on Sunday mornings.

"The way we did it in those days was meet for breakfast in the hotel. We started with 8, 9, or 10 guys. Before the year was over, we had maybe 15 coming. When I was traded (to the Cardinals), we were having around 20 at breakfast. From that beginning, Baseball Chapel has grown to an extent where today there are 26 major league teams, and all 26 teams have Sunday morning chapel."

The focus of the program, continued Kessinger, is to provide a regular time and place for players to gather together for a time of prayer, praise, and teaching.

"That's the object of the thing in the first place; they figured when we were away from home we didn't have the opportunity to attend the church of our choice because we have to be at the ball park so early, and usually, after the game on Sunday, we're flying somewhere else."

Kessinger went on to explain how Jesus Christ, through such channels as the Baseball Chapel program, brings into his life fullness and balance.

"It tends to put a person's priorities in the right place," he noted. "It makes me realize that as important as baseball is to me, and as much as I want to win, if I go out there and go oh-for-four today, it's not my life; it has nothing to do with my family. It's my business. I believe that God teaches us that when you work for somebody, you work for him as if he was Jesus Christ really. You're supposed to perform your task as if Christ was watching you all the time, which He is. So you put everything you have into it."

Yet, he added firmly, God is not going to demand anything more than He can offer.

"I believe that you put everything you have into it. But once you've prepared yourself mentally and physically and gone out and played the best you could, if you have a bad day that day, you just had a bad day. That man out there on the mound may be a Christian, too. As far as saying if a man becomes a Christian he's going to go out and hit .330, that's just not the way it works. My prayer is that the Lord would let me perform to the best of my ability and praise His name for whatever the results are. And that's sometimes a difficult prayer to utter when you struck out with the bases loaded, it really is."

Kessinger has had opportunities to convey ideas such as these to young people who attend his sports camp in Braggadocio, Missouri. The camp, begun in 1977, is open to youngsters who wish to increase their skills in either baseball or basketball.

Kessinger, with the assistance of a friend, Max Redmond, purchased an unused school building and then developed it into a facility for youngsters. The camp includes dormitories, a lounge, and a cafeteria, along with a gymnasium, outdoor basketball courts, indoor pitching machines and even videotape equipment to help in the development of a young athlete. Kessinger explained that youngsters may find the camp to be somewhat different from other such programs.

"We have a unique situation there," he observed. "We truly do want the kid who comes to our camp to be the most important thing in mind, and obviously we want him to get his money's worth. We want to teach him everything about the particular sport he's coming for, whether it's basketball or baseball. But at the same time we would like to be able to share quite a bit about life with him while he's there, just in the way you live your life and the way you treat people. We have some films that we show at the camp, one having to do with my family, put together by the Fellowship of Christian Athletes and the Southern Baptist Convention. The one on my life naturally shares my Christian experience with them, so the people there see that. The people who are involved in the camp are Christians, and we would just like to share our way of life with others, but we're not trying to push our way of life on anybody. We just think we have the far better way to live and we have Something greater than us guiding us. We would like for people, when they leave there, to at least realize there's something different about our camp."

The Arkansas native feels honored that God would choose to work through his talents to touch others. "I think that's what everybody would deep down like to do, to be able to use whatever influence he has for good, channel it the right way."

Kessinger, who also operates raquetball clubs, is naturally kept busy by all of his commitments. Yet, he treasures the moments he can spend with his family. The seasoned major-leaguer lives in Memphis, Tennessee, with his wife Carolyn and sons, Keith and Kevin. Kessinger expressed his gratitude to God for his family. Prior to the opening of the 1979 baseball season, Kessinger was named player-manager of the Chicago White Sox.

"I'm just a very fortunate man. You'll never meet a finer Christian lady than my wife. I have an extremely fine family, which we really and truly try to put Christ at the head of. They've supported me in everything I've done. Baseball's a very difficult life on a wife and family. There's a great deal of love between us, and I think I'm very close to my wife and my kids, and I think that's because we put Christ at the head of our family. I truly believe that it's not the quantity of time you spend with your family, it's the quality of time. My children realize that when I have the time, it's theirs."

Thus Kessinger, realizing what is most important to him, will continue to serve God, both on the field and by caring for his family. The veteran infielder closed on a comforting note, explaining that while his children and other youngsters are being exposed to attitudes and influences which may at times block the light of God, brightness is nevertheless penetrating the world.

"Just as today people are more open immorally, Christians today are more outspoken. I believe that. It's a time you take a stand today. You don't just try to go down the middle of the road like you used to. You kind of take a stand, and fortunately, I think I'm on the winning side."